LEGAL ETHICS FOR EVERYDAY PRACTICE

NICHOLAS PALEVEDA MBA J.D. LL.M

ADJUNCT PROFESSOR, GRADUATE TAX PROGRAM NORTHEASTERN
UNIVERSITY, BOSTON SPRING 2012

Legal Ethics for Everyday Practice

ETHICAL CLIENT COMMUNICATIONS

- Protecting Confidentiality
- Preventing Conflicts of Interest
- Keeping the Client in the Loop
- Admitting to the Client When You've Made a Mistake
- Managing Difficult Clients
- What to do When Co-Clients are Fighting?
- Representing a Mentally Incapable Client or a Minor
- Implied Attorney-Client Contracts

RESPONSIBLE MANAGEMENT OF ATTORNEY FEES AND CLIENT TRUST ACCOUNTS

- Choosing the Appropriate Billing Method
- Initial Fee Agreements
- Simple Tips to Avoid Commingling of Funds
- Keeping Impeccable Financial Records
- How to Write Invoices That Clients Will Pay
- Fee Splitting
- Resolving Fee Disputes

RECORD-KEEPING PRACTICES THAT PREVENT LEGAL MALPRACTICE ALLEGATIONS

- How Long do I Keep the Closed Case File?
- What Must Be Done When a Lawyer Enters or Leaves the Firm?
- Electronic Communications Challenges
- Can an Attorney Secretly Record Conversations?

PREVENTING LEGAL MALPRACTICE IN EVERYDAY PRACTICE

- Interstate Practice of Law
- Partnering with Colleagues and Case Referral
- Ethical Advertising and the Pitfalls in Online Marketing
- Assisting a Pro Se Litigant
- Unauthorized Practice of Law - What to do When You're in Way Over Your Head
- Hidden Dangers of Office Sharing Arrangements

About the Author:

Nick Paleveda is an Adjunct Professor for the Graduate Tax Program at Northeastern University in Boston and CEO of National Pension Partners. Mr. Paleveda received his B.A. in 1977 and M.B.A. degree in 1979 from the University of South Florida. Mr. Paleveda received his J.D from the University of Miami in 1982 and received his Master of Laws in Taxation from the University of Denver in 1983. Mr. Paleveda attended summer law programs at Oxford University and business programs at Harvard University. In 1984 he was admitted to practice law in the State of Florida, admitted before the U.S. Tax Court, and admitted before the 11th Circuit Court of Appeals. In 1984 Mr. Paleveda founded the law firm Hampton, Paleveda, Murphy, Cody and Levy. Mr. Paleveda left the firm in 1987 to join Mutual Benefit Life until 1993. While at Mutual Benefit Life, Mr. Paleveda conducted over 1,000 Advanced Tax and Estate Planning Seminars throughout the U.S. in almost every major city. Mr. Paleveda's client list included; the founder of Dunkin Donuts, the President of Phillip Morris, the President of Kimberly-Clarke, the founding family of Coca-Cola and others. In 1993 Mr. Paleveda returned to law practice at the firm of Paleveda and Rome. In 1997 Mr. Paleveda became a contributing author for "The Life Insurance Answer Book for Qualified Plans and Estate Planning" and was appointed the Adjunct Professor for Retirement Planning for the College for Financial Planning at Oglethorpe University in Atlanta. In 2001 Mr. Paleveda became a CEO for a pension administration firm in Seattle Washington. In 2006, Mr. Paleveda became CEO for a pension consulting firm in Bellingham Washington and in 2010, the President of National Pension Partners. Mr. Paleveda is a USCF chess master and the Florida State Chess Champion in 1977, 1978 and 1994. He was a top 10 player in Chess nationally in high school and in college. In Trivia, his Team won the Whatcom County Championship two years in a row. (One year with the help of Ken Jennings). Mr. Paleveda is a member the American Bar Association and Infinity International Society Top 99.63% in psychometric testing. In 2009, Mr. Paleveda was admitted to practice before the 9th Circuit Court of Appeals and the Supreme Court of the United States. In 2011, Mr. Paleveda became an Adjunct Professor for the Masters in Taxation Program at Northeastern University in Boston as lead faculty for the Retirement Planning Courses. He can be reached at Nick@nationalpensions.com

Contents

ISBN 13: 978-1478113195

ISBN 10: 1478113197

Protecting Confidentiality

The ethical rules differ from state to state. The American Bar Association has adopted model rules concerning confidentiality of information. Each individual must review their state rules as to the language and interpretation of these rules. Most of this work is taken from the ABA model rules of professional responsibility and case law in the area, hence it is "substantial authority" except where the author expresses his opinions.

Model Rules from the American Bar Association

Rule 1.6 Confidentiality of Information

(a) A lawyer shall not reveal information relating to the representation of a client unless the client gives informed consent, the disclosure is impliedly authorized in order to carry out the representation or the disclosure is permitted by paragraph (b).

(b) A lawyer may reveal information relating to the representation of a client to the extent the lawyer reasonably believes necessary:

(1) to prevent reasonably certain death or substantial bodily harm;

(2) to prevent the client from committing a crime or fraud that is reasonably certain to result in substantial injury to the financial interests or property of another and in furtherance of which the client has used or is using the lawyer's services;

(3) to prevent, mitigate or rectify substantial injury to the financial interests or property of another that is reasonably certain to result or has resulted from the client's commission of a crime or fraud in furtherance of which the client has used the lawyer's services;

(4) to secure legal advice about the lawyer's compliance with these Rules;

(5) to establish a claim or defense on behalf of the lawyer in a controversy between the lawyer and the client, to establish a defense to a criminal charge or civil claim against the lawyer based upon conduct in which the client was involved, or to respond to allegations in any proceeding concerning the lawyer's representation of the client; or

(6) to comply with other law or a court order.

Rule 1.6 Confidentiality of Information - Comment

This Rule governs the disclosure by a lawyer of information relating to the representation of a client during the lawyer's representation of the client. See Rule 1.18 for the lawyer's duties with respect to information provided to the lawyer by a prospective client, Rule 1.9(c) (2) for the lawyer's duty not to reveal information relating to the lawyer's prior representation of a former client and Rules 1.8(b) and 1.9(c) (1) for the lawyer's duties with respect to the use of such information to the disadvantage of clients and former clients.

A fundamental principle in the client-lawyer relationship is that, in the absence of the client's informed consent, the lawyer must not reveal information relating to the representation. See Rule 1.0(e) for the definition of informed consent. This contributes to the trust that is the hallmark of the client-lawyer relationship. The client is thereby encouraged to seek legal assistance and to communicate fully and frankly with the lawyer even as to embarrassing or legally damaging subject matter. The lawyer needs this information to represent the client effectively and, if necessary, to advise the client to refrain from wrongful conduct. Almost without exception, clients come to lawyers in order to determine their rights and what is, in the complex of laws and regulations, deemed to be legal and correct. Based upon experience, lawyers know that almost all clients follow the advice given, and the law is upheld.

he principle of client-lawyer confidentiality is given effect by related bodies of law: the attorney-client privilege, the work product doctrine and the rule of confidentiality established in professional ethics. The attorney-client privilege and work-product doctrine apply in judicial and other proceedings in which a lawyer may be called as a witness or otherwise required to produce evidence concerning a client. The rule of client-lawyer confidentiality applies in situations other than those where evidence is sought from the lawyer through compulsion of law. The confidentiality rule, for example, applies not only to matters communicated in confidence by the client but also to all information relating to the representation, whatever its source. A lawyer may not disclose such information except as authorized or required by the Rules of Professional Conduct or other law. See also Scope.

Paragraph (a) prohibits a lawyer from revealing information relating to the representation of a client. This prohibition also applies to disclosures by a lawyer that do not in themselves reveal protected information but could reasonably lead to the discovery of such information by a third person. A lawyer's use of a hypothetical to discuss issues relating to the representation is permissible so long as there is no reasonable likelihood that the listener will be able to ascertain the identity of the client or the situation involved.

Authorized Disclosure

Except to the extent that the client's instructions or special circumstances limit that authority, a lawyer is impliedly authorized to make disclosures about a client when appropriate in carrying out the representation. In some situations, for example, a lawyer may be impliedly authorized to admit a fact that cannot properly be disputed or to make a disclosure that facilitates a satisfactory conclusion to a matter. Lawyers in a firm may, in the course of the firm's practice, disclose to each other information relating to a client of the firm, unless the client has instructed that particular information be confined to specified lawyers.

Disclosure Adverse to Client

Although the public interest is usually best served by a strict rule requiring lawyers to preserve the confidentiality of information relating to the representation of their clients, the confidentiality rule is subject to limited exceptions. Paragraph (b) (1) recognizes the overriding value of life and physical integrity and permits disclosure reasonably necessary to prevent reasonably certain death or substantial bodily harm. Such harm is reasonably certain to occur if it will be suffered imminently or if there is a present and substantial threat that a person will suffer such harm at a later date if the lawyer fails to take action necessary to eliminate the threat. Thus, a lawyer who knows that a client has accidentally discharged toxic waste into a town's water supply may reveal this information to the authorities if there is a present and substantial risk that a person who drinks the water will contract a life-threatening or debilitating disease and the lawyer's disclosure is necessary to eliminate the threat or reduce the number of victims.

Paragraph (b) (2) is a limited exception to the rule of confidentiality that permits the lawyer to reveal information to the extent necessary to enable affected persons or appropriate authorities to prevent the client from committing a crime or fraud, as defined in Rule 1.0(d), that is reasonably certain to result in substantial injury to the financial or property interests of another and in furtherance of which the client has used or is using the lawyer's services. Such a serious abuse of the client-lawyer relationship by the client forfeits the protection of this Rule. The client can, of course, prevent such disclosure by refraining from the wrongful conduct. Although paragraph (b) (2) does not require the lawyer to reveal the client's misconduct, the lawyer may not counsel or assist the client in conduct the lawyer knows is criminal or fraudulent. See Rule 1.2(d). See also Rule 1.16 with respect to the lawyer's obligation or right to withdraw from the representation of the client in such circumstances, and Rule 1.13(c), which permits the lawyer, where the client is an organization, to reveal information relating to the representation in limited circumstances.

Paragraph (b) (3) addresses the situation in which the lawyer does not learn of the client's crime or fraud until after it has been consummated. Although the client no longer has the option of preventing disclosure by refraining from the wrongful conduct, there will be situations in which the loss suffered by the affected person can be prevented, rectified or mitigated. In such situations, the lawyer may disclose information relating to the representation to the extent necessary to enable the affected persons to prevent or mitigate reasonably certain losses or to attempt to recoup their losses. Paragraph (b) (3) does not apply when a person who has committed a crime or fraud thereafter employs a lawyer for representation concerning that offense.

A lawyer's confidentiality obligations do not preclude a lawyer from securing confidential legal advice about the lawyer's personal responsibility to comply with these Rules. In most situations, disclosing information to secure such advice will be impliedly authorized for the lawyer to carry out the representation. Even when the disclosure is not impliedly authorized, paragraph (b) (4) permits such disclosure because of the importance of a lawyer's compliance with the Rules of Professional Conduct.

Where a legal claim or disciplinary charge alleges complicity of the lawyer in a client's conduct or other misconduct of the lawyer involving representation of the client, the lawyer may respond to the extent the lawyer reasonably believes necessary to establish a defense. The same is true with respect to a claim involving the conduct or representation of a former client. Such a charge can arise in a civil, criminal, disciplinary or other proceeding and can be based on a wrong allegedly committed by the lawyer against the client or on a wrong alleged by a third person, for example, a person claiming to have been defrauded by the lawyer and client acting together. The lawyer's right to respond arises when an assertion of such complicity has been made. Paragraph (b)(5) does not require the lawyer to await the commencement of an action or proceeding that charges such complicity, so that the defense may be established by responding directly to a third party who has made such an assertion. The right to defend also applies, of course, where a proceeding has been commenced.

A lawyer entitled to a fee is permitted by paragraph (b) (5) to prove the services rendered in an action to collect it. This aspect of the rule expresses the principle that the beneficiary of a fiduciary relationship may not exploit it to the detriment of the fiduciary.

Other law may require that a lawyer disclose information about a client. Whether such a law supersedes Rule 1.6 is a question of law beyond the scope of these Rules. When disclosure of information relating to the representation appears to be required by other law, the lawyer must discuss the matter with the client to the extent required by Rule 1.4. If, however, the other law supersedes this Rule and requires disclosure, paragraph (b) (6) permits the lawyer to make such disclosures as are necessary to comply with the law.

A lawyer may be ordered to reveal information relating to the representation of a client by a court or by another tribunal or governmental entity claiming authority pursuant to other law to compel the disclosure. Absent informed consent of the client to do otherwise, the lawyer should assert on behalf of the client all nonfrivolous claims that the order is not authorized by other law or that the information sought is protected against disclosure by the attorney-client privilege or other applicable law. In the event of an adverse ruling, the lawyer must consult with the client about the possibility of appeal to the extent required by Rule 1.4. Unless review is sought, however, paragraph (b) (6) permits the lawyer to comply with the court's order.

Paragraph (b) permits disclosure only to the extent the lawyer reasonably believes the disclosure is necessary to accomplish one of the purposes specified. Where practicable, the lawyer should first seek to persuade the client to take suitable action to obviate the need for disclosure. In any case, a disclosure adverse to the client's interest should be no greater than the lawyer reasonably believes necessary to accomplish the purpose. If the disclosure will be made in connection with a judicial proceeding, the disclosure should be made in a manner that limits access to the information to the tribunal or other persons having a need to know it and appropriate protective orders or other arrangements should be sought by the lawyer to the fullest extent practicable.

Paragraph (b) permits but does not require the disclosure of information relating to a client's representation to accomplish the purposes specified in paragraphs (b)(1) through (b)(6). In exercising the discretion conferred by this Rule, the lawyer may consider such factors as the nature of the lawyer's relationship with the client and with those who might be injured by the client, the lawyer's own involvement in the transaction and factors that may extenuate the conduct in question. A lawyer's decision not to disclose as permitted by paragraph (b) does not violate this Rule. Disclosure may be required, however, by other Rules. Some Rules require disclosure only if such disclosure would be permitted by paragraph (b). See Rules 1.2(d), 4.1(b), 8.1 and 8.3. Rule 3.3, on the other hand, requires disclosure in some circumstances regardless of whether such disclosure is permitted by this Rule. See Rule 3.3(c).

Acting Competently to Preserve Confidentiality

A lawyer must act competently to safeguard information relating to the representation of a client against inadvertent or unauthorized disclosure by the lawyer or other persons who are participating in the representation of the client or who are subject to the lawyer's supervision. See Rules 1.1, 5.1 and 5.3.

When transmitting a communication that includes information relating to the representation of a client, the lawyer must take reasonable precautions to prevent the information from coming into the hands of unintended recipients. This duty, however, does not require that the lawyer use special security measures if the method of communication affords a reasonable expectation of privacy. Special circumstances, however, may warrant special precautions. Factors to be considered in determining the reasonableness of the lawyer's expectation of confidentiality include the sensitivity of the information and the extent to which the privacy of the communication is protected by law or by a confidentiality agreement. A client may require the lawyer to implement special security measures not required by this Rule or may give informed consent to the use of a means of communication that would otherwise be prohibited by this Rule.

Former Client

The duty of confidentiality continues after the client-lawyer relationship has terminated. See Rule 1.9(c) (2). See Rule 1.9(c) (1) for the prohibition against using such information to the disadvantage of the former client.

Preventing Conflicts of Interest

Although much is written on attorney conflict of interest, in many cases you may encounter an arbitrator who has a conflict of interest and does not disclose the conflict. An arbitrator has great discretion as to law and fact. The arbitrator can also be from the well known American Arbitration Association and outstanding member of the local bar. This does not mean you should assume the arbitrator is not hiding a conflict. In a recent case in Washington, an American Arbitration Association Attorney had a 300+ page document showing that the defendant in the case was a former client of the firm or had a substantial relationship with the firm for 19 month. The firm even took possession and title to his personal residence. The defendant was a convicted disbarred attorney who converted a check to himself and others of over $140,000 from a company. The arbitrator took the arbitration anyway without disclosing the conflict and held for his client even awarding his client an additional nearly $100,000 in attorney's fees. Upon discovering the conflict and filing a complaint with the Washington Bar, the Bar Association dismissed the complaint. The company was forced into bankruptcy and the convicted disbarred felon walked away with a huge amount of cash. The arbitrator kept his $16,000.00 fee. In Re: Scott Easter of Montgomery Purdue Blankenship and Austin, Seattle.

The moral of this story-do not trust the arbitrator. AAA does not provide protection and some bar associations will do nothing. Another case of Arbitrator conflict can be found in Positive Software v. New Century Mortgage.

Rule 1.7 Conflict Of Interest: Current Clients

(a) Except as provided in paragraph (b), a lawyer shall not represent a client if the representation involves a concurrent conflict of interest. A concurrent conflict of interest exists if:

(1) the representation of one client will be directly adverse to another client; or

(2) there is a significant risk that the representation of one or more clients will be materially limited by the lawyer's responsibilities to another client, a former client or a third person or by a personal interest of the lawyer.

(b) Notwithstanding the existence of a concurrent conflict of interest under paragraph (a), a lawyer may represent a client if:

(1) the lawyer reasonably believes that the lawyer will be able to provide competent and diligent representation to each affected client;

(2) the representation is not prohibited by law;

(3) the representation does not involve the assertion of a claim by one client against another client represented by the lawyer in the same litigation or other proceeding before a tribunal; and

(4) each affected client gives informed consent, confirmed in writing.

Comment

General Principles

Loyalty and independent judgment are essential elements in the lawyer's relationship to a client. Concurrent conflicts of interest can arise from the lawyer's responsibilities to another client, a former client or a third person or from the lawyer's own interests. For specific Rules regarding certain concurrent conflicts of interest, see Rule 1.8. For former client conflicts of interest, see Rule 1.9. For conflicts of interest involving prospective clients, see Rule 1.18. For definitions of "informed consent" and "confirmed in writing," see Rule 1.0(e) and (b).

Resolution of a conflict of interest problem under this Rule requires the lawyer to: 1) clearly identify the client or clients; 2) determine whether a conflict of interest exists; 3) decide whether the representation may be undertaken despite the existence of a conflict, i.e., whether the conflict is consentable; and 4) if so, consult with the clients affected under paragraph (a) and obtain their informed consent, confirmed in writing. The clients affected under paragraph (a) include both of the clients referred to in paragraph (a) (1) and the one or more clients whose representation might be materially limited under paragraph (a) (2).

A conflict of interest may exist before representation is undertaken, in which event the representation must be declined, unless the lawyer obtains the informed consent of each client under the conditions of paragraph (b). To determine whether a conflict of interest exists, a lawyer should adopt reasonable procedures, appropriate for the size and type of firm and practice, to determine in both litigation and non-litigation matters the persons and issues involved. See also

Comment to Rule 5.1. Ignorance caused by a failure to institute such procedures will not excuse a lawyer's violation of this Rule. As to whether a client-lawyer relationship exists or, having once been established, is continuing, see Comment to Rule 1.3 and Scope.

If a conflict arises after representation has been undertaken, the lawyer ordinarily must withdraw from the representation, unless the lawyer has obtained the informed consent of the client under the conditions of paragraph (b). See Rule 1.16. Where more than one client is involved, whether the lawyer may continue to represent any of the clients is determined both by the lawyer's ability to comply with duties owed to the former client and by the lawyer's ability to represent adequately the remaining client or clients, given the lawyer's duties to the former client. See Rule 1.9. See also Comments [5] and [29].

Unforeseeable developments, such as changes in corporate and other organizational affiliations or the addition or realignment of parties in litigation, might create conflicts in the midst of a representation, as when a company sued by the lawyer on behalf of one client is bought by another client represented by the lawyer in an unrelated matter. Depending on the circumstances, the lawyer may have the option to withdraw from one of the representations in order to avoid the conflict. The lawyer must seek court approval where necessary and take steps to minimize harm to the clients. See Rule 1.16. The lawyer must continue to protect the confidences of the client from whose representation the lawyer has withdrawn. See Rule 1.9(c).

Identifying Conflicts of Interest: Directly Adverse

Loyalty to a current client prohibits undertaking representation directly adverse to that client without that client's informed consent. Thus, absent consent, a lawyer may not act as an advocate in one matter against a person the lawyer represents in some other matter, even when the matters are wholly unrelated. The client as to whom the representation is directly adverse is likely to feel betrayed, and the resulting damage to the client-lawyer relationship is likely to impair the lawyer's ability to represent the client effectively. In addition, the client on whose behalf the adverse representation is undertaken reasonably may fear that the lawyer will pursue that client's case less effectively out of deference to the other client, i.e., that the representation may be materially limited by the lawyer's interest in retaining the current client. Similarly, a directly adverse conflict may arise when a lawyer is required to cross-examine a client who appears as a witness in a lawsuit involving another client, as when the testimony will be damaging to the client who is represented in the lawsuit. On the other hand, simultaneous representation in unrelated matters of clients whose interests are only economically adverse, such as representation of competing economic enterprises in unrelated litigation, does not ordinarily constitute a conflict of interest and thus may not require consent of the respective clients.

Directly adverse conflicts can also arise in transactional matters. For example, if a lawyer is asked to represent the seller of a business in negotiations with a buyer represented by the lawyer, not in the same transaction but in another, unrelated matter, the lawyer could not undertake the representation without the informed consent of each client.

Identifying Conflicts of Interest: Material Limitation

Even where there is no direct adverseness, a conflict of interest exists if there is a significant risk that a lawyer's ability to consider, recommend or carry out an appropriate course of action for the client will be materially limited as a result of the lawyer's other responsibilities or interests. For example, a lawyer asked to represent several individuals seeking to form a joint venture is likely to be materially limited in the lawyer's ability to recommend or advocate all possible positions that each might take because of the lawyer's duty of loyalty to the others. The conflict in effect forecloses alternatives that would otherwise be available to the client. The mere possibility of subsequent harm does not itself require disclosure and consent. The critical questions are the likelihood that a difference in interests will eventuate and, if it does, whether it will materially interfere with the lawyer's independent professional judgment in considering alternatives or foreclose courses of action that reasonably should be pursued on behalf of the client.

Lawyer's Responsibilities to Former Clients and Other Third Persons

In addition to conflicts with other current clients, a lawyer's duties of loyalty and independence may be materially limited by responsibilities to former clients under Rule 1.9 or by the lawyer's responsibilities to other persons, such as fiduciary duties arising from a lawyer's service as a trustee, executor or corporate director.

Personal Interest Conflicts

The lawyer's own interests should not be permitted to have an adverse effect on representation of a client. For example, if the probity of a lawyer's own conduct in a transaction is in serious question, it may be difficult or impossible for the lawyer to give a client detached advice. Similarly, when a lawyer has discussions concerning possible employment with an opponent of the lawyer's client or with a law firm representing the opponent, such discussions could materially limit the lawyer's representation of the client. In addition, a lawyer may not allow related business interests to affect representation, for example, by referring clients to an enterprise in which the lawyer has an undisclosed financial interest. See Rule 1.8 for specific Rules pertaining to a number of personal interest conflicts, including business transactions with clients. See also Rule 1.10 (personal interest conflicts under Rule 1.7 ordinarily are not imputed to other lawyers in a law firm).

When lawyers representing different clients in the same matter or in substantially related matters are closely related by blood or marriage, there may be a significant risk that client confidences will be revealed and that the lawyer's family relationship will interfere with both loyalty and independent professional judgment. As a result, each client is entitled to know of the existence and implications of the relationship between the lawyers before the lawyer agree to undertake the representation. Thus, a lawyer related to another lawyer, e.g., as parent, child, sibling or spouse, ordinarily may not represent a client in a matter where that lawyer is representing another party, unless each client gives informed consent. The disqualification arising from a close family relationship is personal and ordinarily is not imputed to members of firms with whom the lawyers are associated. See Rule 1.10.

A lawyer is prohibited from engaging in sexual relationships with a client unless the sexual relationship predates the formation of the client-lawyer relationship. See Rule 1.8(j).

Interest of Person Paying for a Lawyer's Service

A lawyer may be paid from a source other than the client, including a co-client, if the client is informed of that fact and consents and the arrangement does not compromise the lawyer's duty of loyalty or independent judgment to the client. See Rule 1.8(f). If acceptance of the payment from any other source presents a significant risk that the lawyer's representation of the client will be materially limited by the lawyer's own interest in accommodating the person paying the lawyer's fee or by the lawyer's responsibilities to a payer who is also a co-client, then the lawyer must comply with the requirements of paragraph (b) before accepting the representation, including determining whether the conflict is consentable and, if so, that the client has adequate information about the material risks of the representation.

Prohibited Representations

Ordinarily, clients may consent to representation notwithstanding a conflict. However, as indicated in paragraph (b), some conflicts are nonconsentable, meaning that the lawyer involved cannot properly ask for such agreement or provide representation on the basis of the client's consent. When the lawyer is representing more than one client, the question of consentability must be resolved as to each client.

Consentability is typically determined by considering whether the interests of the clients will be adequately protected if the clients are permitted to give their informed consent to representation burdened by a conflict of interest. Thus, under paragraph (b) (1), representation is prohibited if in the circumstances the lawyer cannot reasonably conclude that the lawyer will be able to provide competent and diligent representation. See Rule 1.1 (competence) and Rule 1.3 (diligence).

Paragraph (b) (2) describes conflicts that are nonconsentable because the representation is prohibited by applicable law. For example, in some states substantive law provides that the same lawyer may not represent more than one defendant in a capital case, even with the consent of the clients, and under federal criminal statutes certain representations by a former government lawyer are prohibited, despite the informed consent of the former client. In addition, decisional law in some states limits the ability of a governmental client, such as a municipality, to consent to a conflict of interest.

Paragraph (b) (3) describes conflicts that are nonconsentable because of the institutional interest in vigorous development of each client's position when the clients are aligned directly against each other in the same litigation or other proceeding before a tribunal. Whether clients are aligned directly against each other within the meaning of this paragraph requires examination of the context of the proceeding. Although this paragraph does not preclude a lawyer's multiple representation of adverse parties to mediation (because mediation is not a proceeding before a "tribunal" under Rule 1.0(m)), such representation may be precluded by paragraph (b) (1).

Informed Consent

Informed consent requires that each affected client be aware of the relevant circumstances and of the material and reasonably foreseeable ways that the conflict could have adverse effects on the interests of that client. See Rule 1.0(e) (informed consent). The information required depends on the nature of the conflict and the nature of the risks involved. When representation of multiple clients in a single matter is undertaken, the information must include the implications of the common representation, including possible effects on loyalty, confidentiality and the attorney-client privilege and the advantages and risks involved. See Comments [30] and [31] (effect of common representation on confidentiality).

Under some circumstances it may be impossible to make the disclosure necessary to obtain consent. For example, when the lawyer represents different clients in related matters and one of the clients refuses to consent to the disclosure necessary to permit the other client to make an informed decision, the lawyer cannot properly ask the latter to consent. In some cases the alternative to common representation can be that each party may have to obtain separate representation with the possibility of incurring additional costs. These costs, along with the benefits of securing separate representation, are factors that may be considered by the affected client in determining whether common representation is in the client's interests.

Consent Confirmed in Writing

Paragraph (b) requires the lawyer to obtain the informed consent of the client, confirmed in writing. Such writing may consist of a document executed by the client or one that the lawyer promptly records and transmits to the client following an oral consent. See Rule 1.0(b). See also Rule 1.0(n) (writing includes electronic transmission). If it is not feasible to obtain or transmit the writing at the time the client gives informed consent, then the lawyer must obtain or transmit it within a reasonable time thereafter. See Rule 1.0(b). The requirement of a writing does not supplant the need in most cases for the lawyer to talk with the client, to explain the risks and advantages, if any, of representation burdened with a conflict of interest, as well as reasonably available alternatives, and to afford the client a reasonable opportunity to consider the risks and alternatives and to raise questions and concerns. Rather, the writing is required in order to impress upon clients the seriousness of the decision the client is being asked to make and to avoid disputes or ambiguities that might later occur in the absence of writing.

Revoking Consent

A client who has given consent to a conflict may revoke the consent and, like any other client, may terminate the lawyer's representation at any time. Whether revoking consent to the client's own representation precludes the lawyer from continuing to represent other clients depends on the circumstances, including the nature of the conflict, whether the client revoked consent because of a material change in circumstances, the reasonable expectations of the other client and whether material detriment to the other clients or the lawyer would result.

Consent to Future Conflict

Whether a lawyer may properly request a client to waive conflicts that might arise in the future is subject to the test of paragraph (b). The effectiveness of such waivers is generally determined by the extent to which the client reasonably understands the material risks that the waiver entails. The more comprehensive the explanation of the types of future representations that might arise and the actual and reasonably foreseeable adverse consequences of those representations, the greater the likelihood that the client will have the requisite understanding. Thus, if the client agrees to consent to a particular type of conflict with which the client is already familiar, then the consent ordinarily will be effective with regard to that type of conflict. If the consent is general and open-ended, then the consent ordinarily will be ineffective, because it is not reasonably likely that the client will have understood the material risks involved. On the other hand, if the client is an experienced user of the legal services involved and is reasonably informed regarding the risk that a conflict may arise, such consent is more likely to be effective, particularly if, e.g., the client is independently represented by other counsel in giving consent and the consent is limited to future conflicts unrelated to the subject of the representation. In any case, advance consent cannot be effective if the circumstances that materialize in the future are such as would make the conflict nonconsentable under paragraph (b).

Conflicts in Litigation

Paragraph (b) (3) prohibits representation of opposing parties in the same litigation, regardless of the clients' consent. On the other hand, simultaneous representation of parties whose interests in litigation may conflict, such as coplaintiffs or codefendants, is governed by paragraph (a) (2). A conflict may exist by reason of substantial discrepancy in the parties' testimony, incompatibility in positions in relation to an opposing party or the fact that there are substantially different possibilities of settlement of the claims or liabilities in question. Such conflicts can arise in criminal cases as well as civil. The potential for conflict of interest in representing multiple defendants in a criminal case is so grave that ordinarily a lawyer should decline to represent more than one codefendant. On the other hand, common representation of persons having similar interests in civil litigation is proper if the requirements of paragraph (b) are met.

Ordinarily a lawyer may take inconsistent legal positions in different tribunals at different times on behalf of different clients. The mere fact that advocating a legal position on behalf of one client might create precedent adverse to the interests of a client represented by the lawyer in an unrelated matter does not create a conflict of interest. A conflict of interest exists, however, if there is a significant risk that a lawyer's action on behalf of one client will materially limit the lawyer's effectiveness in representing another client in a different case; for example, when a decision favoring one client will create a precedent likely to seriously weaken the position taken on behalf of the other client. Factors relevant in determining whether the clients need to be advised of the risk include: where the cases are pending, whether the issue is substantive or procedural, the temporal relationship between the matters, the significance of the issue to the immediate and long-term interests of the clients involved and the clients' reasonable expectations in retaining the lawyer. If there is significant risk of material limitation, then absent informed consent of the affected clients, the lawyer must refuse one of the representations or withdraw from one or both matters.

When a lawyer represents or seeks to represent a class of plaintiffs or defendants in a class-action lawsuit, unnamed members of the class are ordinarily not considered to be clients of the lawyer for purposes of applying paragraph (a)(1) of this Rule. Thus, the lawyer does not typically need to get the consent of such a person before representing a client suing the person in an unrelated matter. Similarly, a lawyer seeking to represent an opponent in a class action does not typically need the consent of an unnamed member of the class whom the lawyer represents in an unrelated matter.

Nonlitigation Conflicts

Conflicts of interest under paragraphs (a) (1) and (a) (2) arise in contexts other than litigation. Relevant factors in determining whether there is significant potential for material limitation include the duration and intimacy of the lawyer's relationship with the client or clients involved, the functions being performed by the lawyer, the likelihood that disagreements will arise and the likely prejudice to the client from the conflict. The question is often one of proximity and degree.

For example, conflict questions may arise in estate planning and estate administration. A lawyer may be called upon to prepare wills for several family members, such as husband and wife, and, depending upon the circumstances, a conflict of interest may be present. In estate administration the identity of the client may be unclear under the law of a particular jurisdiction. Under one view, the client is the fiduciary; under another view the client is the estate or trust, including its beneficiaries. In order to comply with conflict of interest rules, the lawyer should make clear the lawyer's relationship to the parties involved.

Whether a conflict is consentable depends on the circumstances. For example, a lawyer may not represent multiple parties to a negotiation whose interests are fundamentally antagonistic to each other, but common representation is permissible where the clients are generally aligned in interest even though there is some difference in interest among them. Thus, a lawyer may seek to establish or adjust a relationship between clients on an amicable and mutually advantageous basis; for example, in helping to organize a business in which two or more clients are entrepreneurs, working out the financial reorganization of an enterprise in which two or more clients have an interest or arranging a property distribution in settlement of an estate. The lawyer seeks to resolve potentially adverse interests by developing the parties' mutual interests. Otherwise, each party might have to obtain separate representation, with the possibility of incurring additional cost, complication or even litigation. Given these and other relevant factors, the clients may prefer that the lawyer act for all of them.

Special Considerations in Common Representation

In considering whether to represent multiple clients in the same matter, a lawyer should be mindful that if the common representation fails because the potentially adverse interests cannot be reconciled, the result can be additional cost, embarrassment and recrimination. Ordinarily, the lawyer will be forced to withdraw from representing all of the clients if the common representation fails. In some situations, the risk of failure is so great that multiple representations are plainly impossible. For example, a lawyer cannot undertake common representation of clients where contentious litigation or negotiations between them are imminent or contemplated. Moreover, because the lawyer is required to be impartial between commonly represented clients, representation of multiple clients is improper when it is unlikely that impartiality can be maintained. Generally, if the relationship between the parties has already assumed antagonism, the possibility that the clients' interests can be adequately served by common representation is not very good. Other relevant factors are whether the lawyer subsequently will represent both parties on a continuing basis and whether the situation involves creating or terminating a relationship between the parties.

A particularly important factor in determining the appropriateness of common representation is the effect on client-lawyer confidentiality and the attorney-client privilege. With regard to the attorney-client privilege, the prevailing rule is that, as between commonly represented clients, the privilege does not attach. Hence, it must be assumed that if litigation eventuates between the clients, the privilege will not protect any such communications, and the clients should be so advised.

As to the duty of confidentiality, continued common representation will almost certainly be inadequate if one client asks the lawyer not to disclose to the other client information relevant to the common representation. This is so because the lawyer has an equal duty of loyalty to each client, and each client has the right to be informed of anything bearing on the representation that might affect that client's interests and the right to expect that the lawyer will use that information to that client's benefit. See Rule 1.4. The lawyer should, at the outset of the common representation and as part of the process of obtaining each client's informed consent, advise each client that information will be shared and that the lawyer will have to withdraw if one client decides that some matter material to the representation should be kept from the other. In limited circumstances, it may be appropriate for the lawyer to proceed with the representation when the clients have agreed, after being properly informed, that the lawyer will keep certain information confidential. For example, the lawyer may reasonably conclude that failure to disclose one client's trade secrets to another client will not adversely affect representation involving a joint venture between the clients and agree to keep that information confidential with the informed consent of both clients.

When seeking to establish or adjust a relationship between clients, the lawyer should make clear that the lawyer's role is not that of partisanship normally expected in other circumstances and, thus, that the clients may be required to assume greater responsibility for decisions than when each client is separately represented. Any limitations on the scope of the representation made necessary as a result of the common representation should be fully explained to the clients at the outset of the representation. See Rule 1.2(c).

Subject to the above limitations, each client in the common representation has the right to loyal and diligent representation and the protection of Rule 1.9 concerning the obligations to a former client. The client also has the right to discharge the lawyer as stated in Rule 1.16.

Organizational Clients

A lawyer who represents a corporation or other organization does not, by virtue of that representation, necessarily represent any constituent or affiliated organization, such as a parent or subsidiary. See Rule 1.13(a). Thus, the lawyer for an organization is not barred from accepting representation adverse to an affiliate in an unrelated matter, unless the circumstances are such that the affiliate should also be considered a client of the lawyer, there is an understanding between the lawyer and the organizational client that the lawyer will avoid representation adverse to the client's affiliates, or the lawyer's obligations to either the organizational client or the new client are likely to limit materially the lawyer's representation of the other client.

A lawyer for a corporation or other organization who is also a member of its board of directors should determine whether the responsibilities of the two roles may conflict. The lawyer may be called on to advise the corporation in matters involving actions of the directors. Consideration should be given to the frequency with which such situations may arise, the potential intensity of the conflict, the effect of the lawyer's resignation from the board and the possibility of the corporation's obtaining legal advice from another lawyer in such situations. If there is material risk that the dual role will compromise the lawyer's independence of professional judgment, the lawyer should not serve as a director or should cease to act as the corporation's lawyer when conflicts of interest arise. The lawyer should advise the other members of the board that in some circumstances matters discussed at board meetings while the lawyer is present in the capacity of director might not be protected by the attorney-client privilege and that conflict of interest considerations might require the lawyer's recusal as a director or might require the lawyer and the lawyer's firm to decline representation of the corporation in a matter.

The Positive Software case may be read in its entirety on the 5th Circuit Court of Appeals website. What is considered "trivial" becomes a matter of opinion. In the case I was involved, a disbarred convicted felon embezzled $140,000+- from a company I was a shareholder. When the company sued him, the case went to arbitration before a so-called neutral. In arbitration, the arbitrator has almost total discretions as to law and fact. Before this arbitrator, we lost the case. After the arbitration we discovered the arbitrators firm had a 19 month relationship with the defendant's law firm (including taking title to his home) and did not disclose it. I filed my first bar complaint ever in 28 years against the attorneys involved in this embezzlement- The result- NOTHING. In Re Scott Easter, I did not see a law firm who at one time owned the defendant's home, and had a 19 month relationship with the defendant and did not disclose a 300 page written document but chose to ignore it-to be "trivial". However, the Washington Bar did think it was trivial and Mr. Easter ruled in favor of his former client and awarded his law firms former client an extra +-$100,000. In essence, his former client a disbarred convicted felon walked away with $140,000 and the attorney arbitrator $16,000. Amazing what some people can get away with in some states. The company went bankrupt as all the funds were diverted to the disbarred convicted felon and all the employees lost their jobs. However see Positive Software where a mortgage company took advantage of a software company. My opinion-beware of arbitrators and especially AAA arbitrators. Do not trust what they say as they are not being held accountable.

UNITED STATES COURT OF APPEALS

FOR THE FIFTH CIRCUIT

No. 04-11432

POSITIVE SOFTWARE SOLUTIONS, INC.,

Plaintiff-Appellee,

versus

NEW CENTURY MORTGAGE CORPORATION;

NEW CENTURY FINANCIAL CORPORATION;

ECONDUIT CORPORATION; THE ANYLOAN COMPANY;

JEFF LEMIEUX; FRANK NESE,

Defendants-Appellants.

Appeal from the United States District Court

for the Northern District Texas, Dallas

No. 3:03-CV-257

Before JONES, Chief Judge, REAVLEY, JOLLY, HIGGINBOTHAM, DAVIS,SMITH, WIENER, BARKSDALE, GARZA, DeMOSS, BENAVIDES, STEWART,DENNIS, CLEMENT, PRADO, and OWEN, Circuit Judges.*

EDITH H. JONES, Chief Judge, joined by JOLLY, HIGGINBOTHAM, DAVIS,SMITH, BARKSDALE, DeMOSS, DENNIS, CLEMENT, PRADO, and OWEN, Circuit Judges:

The court reconsidered this case en banc in order to

determine whether an arbitration award must be vacated for "evident partiality," 9 U.S.C. § 10(a)(2), where an arbitrator failed to disclose a prior professional association with a member of one of the law firms that engaged him. We conclude that the Federal Arbitration Act ("FAA") does not mandate the extreme remedy of vacatur for nondisclosure of a trivial past association, and we reverse the district court's contrary judgment, but it is necessary to remand for consideration of appellee's other objections to the arbitral award.

* Circuit Judge KING did not participate in the decision.

Keeping The Client in the Loop

Suspensions have been given to attorneys who have not kept their client informed of the progress of the case. Clients can be demanding, hence in many cases an attorney should have hourly billing or blended billing along with the flat fee to take into account this rule.

Rule 1.4 Communication

(a) A lawyer shall:

(1) promptly inform the client of any decision or circumstance with respect to which the client's informed consent, as defined in Rule 1.0(e), is required by these Rules;

(2) reasonably consult with the client about the means by which the client's objectives are to be accomplished;

(3) keep the client reasonably informed about the status of the matter;

(4) promptly comply with reasonable requests for information; and

(5) consult with the client about any relevant limitation on the lawyer's conduct when the lawyer knows that the client expects assistance not permitted by the Rules of Professional Conduct or other law.

(b) A lawyer shall explain a matter to the extent reasonably necessary to permit the client to make informed decisions regarding the representation.

Rule 1.4 Communication - Comment

Reasonable communication between the lawyer and the client is necessary for the client effectively to participate in the representation.

Communicating with Client

If these Rules require that a particular decision about the representation be made by the client, paragraph (a)(1) requires that the lawyer promptly consult with and secure the client's consent prior to taking action unless prior discussions with the client have resolved what action the client wants the lawyer to take. For example, a lawyer who receives from opposing counsel an offer of settlement in a civil controversy or a proffered plea bargain in a criminal case must promptly inform the client of its substance unless the client has previously indicated that the proposal will be acceptable or unacceptable or has authorized the lawyer to accept or to reject the offer. See Rule 1.2(a).

Paragraph (a) (2) requires the lawyer to reasonably consult with the client about the means to be used to accomplish the client's objectives. In some situations — depending on both the importance of the action under consideration and the feasibility of consulting with the client — this duty will require consultation prior to taking action. In other circumstances, such as during a trial when an immediate decision must be made, the exigency of the situation may require the lawyer to act without prior consultation. In such cases the lawyer must nonetheless act reasonably to inform the client of actions the lawyer has taken on the client's behalf. Additionally, paragraph (a) (3) requires that the lawyer keep the client reasonably informed about the status of the matter, such as significant developments affecting the timing or the substance of the representation.

A lawyer's regular communication with clients will minimize the occasions on which a client will need to request information concerning the representation. When a client makes a reasonable request for information, however, paragraph (a)(4) requires prompt compliance with the request, or if a prompt response is not feasible, that the lawyer, or a member of the lawyer's staff, acknowledge receipt of the request and advise the client when a response may be expected. Client telephone calls should be promptly returned or acknowledged.

Explaining Matters

The client should have sufficient information to participate intelligently in decisions concerning the objectives of the representation and the means by which they are to be pursued; to the extent the client is willing and able to do so. Adequacy of communication depends in part on the kind of advice or assistance that is involved. For example, when there is time to explain a proposal made in a negotiation, the lawyer should review all important provisions with the client before proceeding to an agreement. In litigation a lawyer should explain the general strategy and prospects of success and ordinarily should consult the client on tactics that are likely to result in significant expense or to injure or coerce others. On the other hand, a lawyer ordinarily will not be expected to describe trial or negotiation strategy in detail. The guiding principle is that the lawyer should fulfill reasonable client expectations for information consistent with the duty to act in the client's best interests, and the client's overall requirements as to the character of representation. In certain circumstances, such as when a lawyer asks a client to consent to a representation affected by a conflict of interest, the client must give informed consent, as defined in Rule 1.0(e).

Ordinarily, the information to be provided is that appropriate for a client who is a comprehending and responsible adult. However, fully informing the client according to this standard may be impracticable, for example, where the client is a child or suffers from diminished capacity. See Rule 1.14. When the client is an organization or group, it is often impossible or inappropriate to inform every one of its members about its legal affairs; ordinarily, the lawyer should address communications to the appropriate officials of the organization. See Rule 1.13. Where many routine matters are involved, a system of limited or occasional reporting may be arranged with the client.

Withholding Information

In some circumstances, a lawyer may be justified in delaying transmission of information when the client would be likely to react imprudently to an immediate communication. Thus, a lawyer might withhold a psychiatric diagnosis of a client when the examining psychiatrist indicates that disclosure would harm the client. A lawyer may not withhold information to serve the lawyer's own interest or convenience or the interests or convenience of another person. Rules or court orders governing litigation may provide that information supplied to a lawyer may not be disclosed to the client. Rule 3.4(c) directs compliance with such rules or orders.

Admitting to the client when you made a mistake

This area can be very challenging to an attorney or a law firm.

Law is generally "opinions", however mistakes do happen.

In some cases, the mistake can be corrected. In other cases, the mistake is detrimental to the client's interest. THE LAWYER'S DUTY TO INFORM HIS CLIENT OF HIS OWN MALPRACTICE by Benjamin P. Cooper is an often cited scholarly work in this area. Lawyers have an obligation to keep their clients informed about a matter and this includes mistakes they may have made *See, e.g.*, N.Y. State Bar Association Ethics Opinion 734 (2000).

In the Colorado Bar Association Formal Opinion 113 (2005) the Colorado Bar discusses the ethical duty of an attorney to disclose errors to clients In the N.Y. City Bar Association Formal Op. 1995-2 (1995). Large firms are not immune from this problem: *see* Leonard v. Dorsey & Whitney L.L.P., 553 F.3d 609 (8th Cir. 2009) Olds v. Donnelly, 696 A.2d 633, 643 (N.J. 1997) The Rules of Professional Conduct require an attorney to notify the client that he or she may have a legal malpractice claim even if notification is against the attorney's own interest. Also see *In re* Tallon, 447 N.Y.S.2d 50, 51 (App. Div. 1982) In this case the attorney had a professional duty to notify his client of his failure to act and of the possible claim his client may thus have against him.

Managing Difficult Clients

The ABA Published a book in this area below is an excerpt from this book by Justice Carole Curtis.

HOW TO HANDLE DIFFICULT CLIENTS – Pointers That Will Help You Stay Sane and Safe

By Justice Carole Curtis

Nearly every lawyer from time to time agrees to take on a difficult client, be it knowingly or unwittingly. Although this client may task nerves to the breaking point, taking certain steps can help avert disagreements and possible malpractice claims.

Lawyers are usually fairly clear about their role in a representation, but that role may appear to be less clear when you're dealing with a difficult client. Your first imperative, then, is to get clear on who does what.

Establish Your Role with the Client

Your role is to analyze a given situation and offer a solution to the problem presented, or a means of achieving the goal the client has presented. Sometimes, there are several possible solutions or means, all of which should be offered to the client. Don't forget that "do nothing" is always a possible solution, too. Your role then is to advise on the consequences of the different courses of action. It is the client's job—and not the lawyer's—to decide which course of action to follow. After all, it is the client's life, or business, or litigation, or estate that's at sake.

Difficult clients, however, are sometimes totally unwilling to make decisions about their legal issues and want the lawyer to do it for them. Do not do it. Let some other influential person in their life help them with the decision. Your job is to help the client understand the choices.

Be Thorough in Your Documentation

Document everything you possibly can, including phone calls, voice-mail messages and e-mail messages. Confirm the client's instructions to you in writing, and confirm your instructions to the client in writing. Include the possible consequences of various courses of action the client may be contemplating. Save messages and instructions in your usual way as part of the permanent record of the file. This is good advice for any representation, but it's especially important for difficult clients. They have a way of turning on the lawyer more often and with more damaging consequences than other clients.

Thus, in this context, documenting means recording sufficient details to assist you in a future disagreement. Remember, a record with insufficient details won't be of much use to you if there's a subsequent dispute over who said what to whom and when. This means you should record at least the following for all exchanges relating to the matter:

• The client's name

• The file name

• Who the contact was with

• The date of the contact

• The nature of the contact (phone call, meeting, voice mail, e-mail or the like)

• How long the contact took

• The details of who said what, including what the lawyer said

• Any instructions given during the contact

Inputting the information into a practice management software program can make this task less cumbersome and more reliable than just jotting it down on paper.

In notes of meetings or conversations, it's especially important to record not only the information the client gave to you, but also the information and advice you gave to the client. In disputes between lawyers and clients, this may be the biggest area of disagreement—and one of the least documented. Moreover, in litigation between the lawyer and client, where there is disagreement about the information provided or the legal advice given to the client and that advice is not documented, courts have often preferred the client's evidence on this issue.

Be Calm and Clear

It requires more patience than usual to deal with difficult clients. You will need to be calm *and* very clear with them about everything. The more information you give in writing—and as early in the representation as possible—the less likely there will be misunderstandings.

Also, explain what they should expect regarding their interactions with you and your staff. Be sure they understand whom to deal with on which issues—for example, whom to call to get certain types of information, and when they need to speak directly to their lawyer and when they can deal with staff instead. Many difficult clients want to deal only with the lawyer at every turn, which is expensive, not very efficient and not often necessary.

Make patience your watchword. Do not let the difficult client turn you into the difficult lawyer, or the unhappy lawyer, or the depressed, yelling or swearing lawyer. If you find you are becoming the difficult lawyer, perhaps it is time to transfer the file to another lawyer.

Include Your Staff in the Plan

Usually, the staff will easily be able to identify the difficult client—they may, in fact, know a client is difficult before you do. But they also need to know the risks of acting for the difficult client, so they can behave in ways that minimize those risks, especially in terms of documenting contacts, instructions or information. Make sure they deal with this client the same way you do, using an extra dose of patience.

However, difficult clients are often much more difficult with the staff than they are with the lawyers. Trust your staff and believe them when they describe the client's behavior. Deal directly and promptly with the client concerning any inappropriate treatment, to ensure that the client understands what the staff's role is in the representation and, more importantly, to ensure that the behavior is not repeated. No client is more important than the people who work for you, so institute a zero tolerance policy on abusive behavior toward your people.

Manage Expectations from the Outset

Some clients' expectations or goals are outside the realm of the services you can provide, or the outcomes you can achieve for them. That's why it's important to have a frank discussion with clients, as early as possible, to identify what their expectations are in retaining a lawyer to deal with this particular issue. While clients' unrealistic expectations take many forms, they fall into the following general categories:

• Expectations about service

• Expectations about time

• Expectations about costs

• Expectations about results

If the client has service expectations that are impossible to meet—such as the lawyer always returning phone calls within 15 minutes or performing significant work for free—be clear from the outset that you cannot provide that level or kind of service. If the client has expectations that are unrealistic or very expensive, such as having the matter concluded on a rushed timeline or all work done by the most senior lawyer on the team, be clear about whether you can meet that expectation, or what alternative will be provided, as well as the costs that will be involved.

Remember, too, the difficult client is also a client who is likely to be unhappy about fees, so you need to establish mutual expectations concerning billing and payment procedures for your services. It's especially important to bill clients with high service expectations frequently and regularly, and to provide as much detail as possible, so they can understand the cost of those expectations.

However, the most essential thing to establish during discussions with clients is what results they want to achieve. Clients who are unlikely to be successful in achieving their goals need to be told that explicitly from the start of the representation, or at the earliest possible moment in the representation. It is far more important to be honest with clients who cannot achieve their goals than it is with clients who can. If the client cannot, or will not, accept your assessment of the matter, perhaps the client should find another lawyer.

About the Author

Justice Carole Curtis sits on the Ontario Court of Justice in Toronto. Previously she was the sole proprietor of the firm Carole Curtis, Barristers and Solicitors, working in all areas of family law for 30 years. An earlier version of this article appeared in *LawPRO Magazine*'s Spring 2004 issue.

What to Do when Co-Clients Are Fighting?

Good Question. The answer varies but generally you would want one of the parties to seek separate representation.

Rule 1.7 Conflict Of Interest: Current Clients

(a) Except as provided in paragraph (b), a lawyer shall not represent a client if the representation involves a concurrent conflict of interest. A concurrent conflict of interest exists if:

(1) the representation of one client will be directly adverse to another client; or

(2) there is a significant risk that the representation of one or more clients will be materially limited by the lawyer's responsibilities to another client, a former client or a third person or by a personal interest of the lawyer.

(b) Notwithstanding the existence of a concurrent conflict of interest under paragraph (a), a lawyer may represent a client if:

(1) the lawyer reasonably believes that the lawyer will be able to provide competent and diligent representation to each affected client;

(2) the representation is not prohibited by law;

(3) the representation does not involve the assertion of a claim by one client against another client represented by the lawyer in the same litigation or other proceeding before a tribunal; and

(4) each affected client gives informed consent, confirmed in writing.

Representing Mentally incapable Client or a Minor

Rule 1.14 Client With Diminished Capacity - Comment

The normal client-lawyer relationship is based on the assumption that the client, when properly advised and assisted, is capable of making decisions about important matters. When the client is a minor or suffers from a diminished mental capacity, however, maintaining the ordinary client-lawyer relationship may not be possible in all respects. In particular, a severely incapacitated person may have no power to make legally binding decisions. Nevertheless, a client with diminished capacity often has the ability to understand, deliberate upon, and reach conclusions about matters affecting the client's own well-being. For example, children as young as five or six years of age, and certainly those of ten or twelve, are regarded as having opinions that are entitled to weight in legal proceedings concerning their custody. So also, it is recognized that some persons of advanced age can be quite capable of handling routine financial matters while needing special legal protection concerning major transactions.

The fact that a client suffers a disability does not diminish the lawyer's obligation to treat the client with attention and respect. Even if the person has a legal representative, the lawyer should as far as possible accord the represented person the status of client, particularly in maintaining communication.

The client may wish to have family members or other persons participate in discussions with the lawyer. When necessary to assist in the representation, the presence of such persons generally does not affect the applicability of the attorney-client evidentiary privilege. Nevertheless, the lawyer must keep the client's interests foremost and, except for protective action authorized under paragraph (b), must to look to the client, and not family members, to make decisions on the client's behalf.

If a legal representative has already been appointed for the client, the lawyer should ordinarily look to the representative for decisions on behalf of the client. In matters involving a minor, whether the lawyer should look to the parents as natural guardians may depend on the type of proceeding or matter in which the lawyer is representing the minor. If the lawyer represents the guardian as distinct from the ward, and is aware that the guardian is acting adversely to the ward's interest, the lawyer may have an obligation to prevent or rectify the guardian's misconduct. See Rule 1.2(d).

Taking Protective Action

If a lawyer reasonably believes that a client is at risk of substantial physical, financial or other harm unless action is taken, and that a normal client-lawyer relationship cannot be maintained as provided in paragraph (a) because the client lacks sufficient capacity to communicate or to make adequately considered decisions in connection with the representation, then paragraph (b) permits the lawyer to take protective measures deemed necessary. Such measures could include: consulting with family members, using a reconsideration period to permit clarification or improvement of circumstances, using voluntary surrogate decisionmaking tools such as durable powers of attorney or consulting with support groups, professional services, adult-protective agencies or other individuals or entities that have the ability to protect the client. In taking any protective action, the lawyer should be guided by such factors as the wishes and values of the client to the extent known, the client's best interests and the goals of intruding into the client's decisionmaking autonomy to the least extent feasible, maximizing client capacities and respecting the client's family and social connections.

In determining the extent of the client's diminished capacity, the lawyer should consider and balance such factors as: the client's ability to articulate reasoning leading to a decision, variability of state of mind and ability to appreciate consequences of a decision; the substantive fairness of a decision; and the consistency of a decision with the known long-term commitments and values of the client. In appropriate circumstances, the lawyer may seek guidance from an appropriate diagnostician.

If a legal representative has not been appointed, the lawyer should consider whether appointment of a guardian ad litem, conservator or guardian is necessary to protect the client's interests. Thus, if a client with diminished capacity has substantial property that should be sold for the client's benefit, effective completion of the transaction may require appointment of a legal representative. In addition, rules of procedure in litigation sometimes provide that minors or persons with diminished capacity must be represented by a guardian or next friend if they do not have a general guardian. In many circumstances, however, appointment of a legal representative may be more expensive or traumatic for the client than circumstances in fact require. Evaluation of such circumstances is a matter entrusted to the professional judgment of the lawyer. In considering alternatives, however, the lawyer should be aware of any law that requires the lawyer to advocate the least restrictive action on behalf of the client.

Disclosure of the Client's Condition

Disclosure of the client's diminished capacity could adversely affect the client's interests. For example, raising the question of diminished capacity could, in some circumstances, lead to proceedings for involuntary commitment. Information relating to the representation is protected by Rule 1.6. Therefore, unless authorized to do so, the lawyer may not disclose such information. When taking protective action pursuant to paragraph (b), the lawyer is impliedly authorized to make the necessary disclosures, even when the client directs the lawyer to the contrary. Nevertheless, given the risks of disclosure, paragraph (c) limits what the lawyer may disclose in consulting with other individuals or entities or seeking the appointment of a legal representative. At the very least, the lawyer should determine whether it is likely that the person or entity consulted with will act adversely to the client's interests before discussing matters related to the client. The lawyer's position in such cases is an unavoidably difficult one.

Emergency Legal Assistance

In an emergency where the health, safety or a financial interest of a person with seriously diminished capacity is threatened with imminent and irreparable harm, a lawyer may take legal action on behalf of such a person even though the person is unable to establish a client-lawyer relationship or to make or express considered judgments about the matter, when the person or another acting in good faith on that person's behalf has consulted with the lawyer. Even in such an emergency, however, the lawyer should not act unless the lawyer reasonably believes that the person has no other lawyer, agent or other representative available. The lawyer should take legal action on behalf of the person only to the extent reasonably necessary to maintain the status quo or otherwise avoid imminent and irreparable harm. A lawyer who undertakes to represent a person in such an exigent situation has the same duties under these Rules as the lawyer would with respect to a client.

A lawyer who acts on behalf of a person with seriously diminished capacity in an emergency should keep the confidences of the person as if dealing with a client, disclosing them only to the extent necessary to accomplish the intended protective action. The lawyer should disclose to any tribunal involved and to any other counsel involved the nature of his or her relationship with the person. The lawyer should take steps to regularize the relationship or implement other protective solutions as soon as possible. Normally, a lawyer would not seek compensation for such emergency actions taken.

Implied Attorney Client Contracts

In Advanced Manufacturing Technologies Inc. v. Motorola Inc., No. CIV99-01219PH XMHMLOA (D. Ariz. July 2, 2002), an attorney represented Motorola Inc. in a dispute over the possible sale of its machine shop to another company. A retired Motorola employee, who had managed the shop, believed that his firm also represented him. And when this was stated in a deposition, the attorney did not correct him. Motorola threatened to sue for talking to the prospective buyer about working with the company after the sale; he tried to disqualify the firm from representing Motorola. The firm responded that he had never represented him but by then it was too late. U.S. Magistrate Judge Lawrence O. Anderson ruled the firm had shared confidential information and had a conflict of interest. The judge allowed the firm to continue representing Motorola, subject to court-imposed safeguards to protect the employee's interests.

If a lawyer isn't careful, someone may inadvertently become an actual client—or think he or she is—often with grave consequences.

The ABA Model Rules of Professional Conduct are silent on the formation of a lawyer-client relationship, the Restatement (Third) of the Law Governing Lawyers provides in section 14 that the relationship is formed when a person manifests an intent that a lawyer provide legal services, and the lawyer either (a) manifests consent or (b) fails to manifest lack of consent and knows or reasonably should know the person reasonably relied on the lawyer to provide the services. In other words, if a person asks a legal question, and a lawyer answers or says he or she will look into it, a lawyer-client relationship may result. There's no need to sign an agreement, shake hands, discuss rates or send an engagement letter. Once a person becomes a client—even inadvertently—it triggers all the obligations of the attorney-client relationship: loyalty, competency, diligence and confidentiality. Further, under ABA Model Rule 1.10, an inadvertent client relationship imputes to the lawyer's firm, not just to the lawyer.

In *Togstad v. Vesely, Otto, Miller & Keefe*, 291 N.W.2d 686 (Minn. 1980), the court upheld nearly $650,000 in judgments against a firm that thought it had declined a representation. The court ruled that an inadvertent lawyer-client relationship had been created, and thus the firm should have advised the plaintiff about the statute of limitations that governed her original claim. Lawyers who aren't careful to avoid inadvertent clients may face malpractice claims, disqualification—or worse

Choosing the Appropriate Billing Method

Rule 1.5 Fees

(a) A lawyer shall not make an agreement for, charge, or collect an unreasonable fee or an unreasonable amount for expenses. The factors to be considered in determining the reasonableness of a fee include the following:

(1) the time and labor required, the novelty and difficulty of the questions involved, and the skill requisite to perform the legal service properly;

(2) the likelihood, if apparent to the client, that the acceptance of the particular employment will preclude other employment by the lawyer;

(3) the fee customarily charged in the locality for similar legal services;

(4) the amount involved and the results obtained;

(5) the time limitations imposed by the client or by the circumstances;

(6) the nature and length of the professional relationship with the client;

(7) the experience, reputation, and ability of the lawyer or lawyers performing the services; and

(8) whether the fee is fixed or contingent.

(b) The scope of the representation and the basis or rate of the fee and expenses for which the client will be responsible shall be communicated to the client, preferably in writing, before or within a reasonable time after commencing the representation, except when the lawyer will charge a regularly represented client on the same basis or rate. Any changes in the basis or rate of the fee or expenses shall also be communicated to the client.

(c) A fee may be contingent on the outcome of the matter for which the service is rendered, except in a matter in which a contingent fee is prohibited by paragraph (d) or other law. A contingent fee agreement shall be in a writing signed by the client and shall state the method by which the fee is to be determined, including the percentage or percentages that shall accrue to the lawyer in the event of settlement, trial or appeal; litigation and other expenses to be deducted from the recovery; and whether such expenses are to be deducted before or after the contingent fee is calculated. The agreement must clearly notify the client of any expenses for which the client will be liable whether or not the client is the prevailing party. Upon conclusion of a contingent fee matter, the lawyer shall provide the client with a written statement stating the outcome of the matter and, if there is a recovery, showing the remittance to the client and the method of its determination.

(d) A lawyer shall not enter into an arrangement for, charge, or collect:

(1) any fee in a domestic relations matter, the payment or amount of which is contingent upon the securing of a divorce or upon the amount of alimony or support, or property settlement in lieu thereof; or

(2) a contingent fee for representing a defendant in a criminal case.

(e) A division of a fee between lawyers who are not in the same firm may be made only if:

(1) the division is in proportion to the services performed by each lawyer or each lawyer assumes joint responsibility for the representation;

(2) the client agrees to the arrangement, including the share each lawyer will receive, and the agreement is confirmed in writing; and

(3) the total fee is reasonable.

Reasonableness of Fee and Expenses

Paragraph (a) requires that lawyers charge fees that are reasonable under the circumstances. The factors specified in (1) through (8) are not exclusive. Nor will each factor be relevant in each instance. Paragraph (a) also requires that expenses for which the client will be charged must be reasonable. A lawyer may seek reimbursement for the cost of services performed in-house, such as copying, or for other expenses incurred in-house, such as telephone charges, either by charging a reasonable amount to which the client has agreed in advance or by charging an amount that reasonably reflects the cost incurred by the lawyer.

Basis or Rate of Fee

When the lawyer has regularly represented a client, they ordinarily will have evolved an understanding concerning the basis or rate of the fee and the expenses for which the client will be responsible. In a new client-lawyer relationship, however, an understanding as to fees and expenses must be promptly established. Generally, it is desirable to furnish the client with at least a simple memorandum or copy of the lawyer's customary fee arrangements that states the general nature of the legal services to be provided, the basis, rate or total amount of the fee and whether and to what extent the client will be responsible for any costs, expenses or disbursements in the course of the representation. A written statement concerning the terms of the engagement reduces the possibility of misunderstanding.

Contingent fees, like any other fees, are subject to the reasonableness standard of paragraph (a) of this Rule. In determining whether a particular contingent fee is reasonable, or whether it is reasonable to charge any form of contingent fee, a lawyer must consider the factors that are relevant under the circumstances. Applicable law may impose limitations on contingent fees, such as a ceiling on the percentage allowable, or may require a lawyer to offer clients an alternative basis for the fee. Applicable law also may apply to situations other than a contingent fee, for example, government regulations regarding fees in certain tax matters.

Terms of Payment

A lawyer may require advance payment of a fee, but is obliged to return any unearned portion. See Rule 1.16(d). A lawyer may accept property in payment for services, such as an ownership interest in an enterprise, providing this does not involve acquisition of a proprietary interest in the cause of action or subject matter of the litigation contrary to Rule 1.8 (i). However, a fee paid in property instead of money may be subject to the requirements of Rule 1.8(a) because such fees often have the essential qualities of a business transaction with the client.

An agreement may not be made whose terms might induce the lawyer improperly to curtail services for the client or perform them in a way contrary to the client's interest. For example, a lawyer should not enter into an agreement whereby services are to be provided only up to a stated amount when it is foreseeable that more extensive services probably will be required, unless the situation is adequately explained to the client. Otherwise, the client might have to bargain for further assistance in the midst of a proceeding or transaction. However, it is proper to define the extent of services in light of the client's ability to pay. A lawyer should not exploit a fee arrangement based primarily on hourly charges by using wasteful procedures.

Prohibited Contingent Fees

Paragraph (d) prohibits a lawyer from charging a contingent fee in a domestic relations matter when payment is contingent upon the securing of a divorce or upon the amount of alimony or support or property settlement to be obtained. This provision does not preclude a contract for a contingent fee for legal representation in connection with the recovery of post-judgment balances due under support, alimony or other financial orders because such contracts do not implicate the same policy concerns.

Division of Fee

A division of fee is a single billing to a client covering the fee of two or more lawyers who are not in the same firm. A division of fee facilitates association of more than one lawyer in a matter in which neither alone could serve the client as well, and most often is used when the fee is contingent and the division is between a referring lawyer and a trial specialist. Paragraph (e) permits the lawyers to divide a fee either on the basis of the proportion of services they render or if each lawyer assumes responsibility for the representation as a whole. In addition, the client must agree to the arrangement, including the share that each lawyer is to receive, and the agreement must be confirmed in writing. Contingent fee agreements must be in a writing signed by the client and must otherwise comply with paragraph (c) of this Rule. Joint responsibility for the representation entails financial and ethical responsibility for the representation as if the lawyers were associated in a partnership. A lawyer should only refer a matter to a lawyer whom the referring lawyer reasonably believes is competent to handle the matter. See Rule 1.1.

Paragraph (e) does not prohibit or regulate division of fees to be received in the future for work done when lawyers were previously associated in a law firm.

Disputes over Fees

If a procedure has been established for resolution of fee disputes, such as an arbitration or mediation procedure established by the bar, the lawyer must comply with the procedure when it is mandatory, and, even when it is voluntary, the lawyer should conscientiously consider submitting to it. Law may prescribe a procedure for determining a lawyer's fee, for example, in representation of an executor or administrator, a class or a person entitled to a reasonable fee as part of the measure of damages. The lawyer entitled to such a fee and a lawyer representing another party concerned with the fee should comply with the prescribed procedure.

Initial Fee Agreement

Lawyers like written agreements. Lawyers like to write or act. If lawyers were good at math, they would be engineers and if they were good at science, they would be medical doctors. So the utility of a written attorney fee agreement seems obvious. A signed writing should remove all doubt about the exact terms of the engagement. In practice, however, the clients like to have you review additional work. A carefully written scope of representation section is in the lawyer's interest because it will ensure that the lawyer is not on the hook for work that is beyond the scope of the agreement.

However, lawyers continue to represent clients without well-written fee agreements or without any fee agreement at all, despite the rules and despite their best interests. It is not uncommon for lawyers to use boilerplate agreements borrowed from other lawyers practicing in the same areas of law—the assumption is that, if it worked once for somebody else, it must be good.

ABA Model Rule 1.5(b) requires that the fee agreement be communicated to the client "preferably in writing" but goes on to state in Rule 1.5(c) that a contingent fee agreement *must* be in writing. California goes further and requires by statute that both contingent fee agreements and most other fee agreements be in writing (Cal. Bus. & Prof. Code §§ 6147 and 6148, respectively). In California, the informed consent of the client is also a factor in determining whether a fee is unconscionable.

Two of the biggest risks inherent in the practice of law are legal malpractice and not getting paid. A well-thought-out and continually reexamined attorney fee agreement is an essential tool for the managing those risks. The fee agreement should be a living document, continually reexamined in light of changes in the law and lessons learned in the lawyer's practice.

Simple Tips to Avoid Commingling of Funds

Rule 1.15 Safekeeping Property - Comment

A lawyer should hold property of others with the care required of a professional fiduciary. Securities should be kept in a safe deposit box, except when some other form of safekeeping is warranted by special circumstances. All property that is the property of clients or third persons, including prospective clients, must be kept separate from the lawyer's business and personal property and, if monies, in one or more trust accounts. Separate trust accounts may be warranted when administering estate monies or acting in similar fiduciary capacities. A lawyer should maintain on a current basis books and records in accordance with generally accepted accounting practice and comply with any recordkeeping rules established by law or court order. See, e.g., Model Rules for Client Trust Account Records.

While normally it is impermissible to commingle the lawyer's own funds with client funds, paragraph (b) provides that it is permissible when necessary to pay bank service charges on that account. Accurate records must be kept regarding which part of the funds are the lawyer's.

Lawyers often receive funds from which the lawyer's fee will be paid. The lawyer is not required to remit to the client funds that the lawyer reasonably believes represent fees owed. However, a lawyer may not hold funds to coerce a client into accepting the lawyer's contention. The disputed portion of the funds must be kept in a trust account and the lawyer should suggest means for prompt resolution of the dispute, such as arbitration. The undisputed portion of the funds shall be promptly distributed.

Paragraph (e) also recognizes that third parties may have lawful claims against specific funds or other property in a lawyer's custody, such as a client's creditor who has a lien on funds recovered in a personal injury action. A lawyer may have a duty under applicable law to protect such third-party claims against wrongful interference by the client. In such cases, when the third-party claim is not frivolous under applicable law, the lawyer must refuse to surrender the property to the client until the claims are resolved. A lawyer should not unilaterally assume to arbitrate a dispute between the client and the third party, but, when there are substantial grounds for dispute as to the person entitled to the funds, the lawyer may file an action to have a court resolve the dispute.

The obligations of a lawyer under this Rule are independent of those arising from activity other than rendering legal services. For example, a lawyer who serves only as an escrow agent is governed by the applicable law relating to fiduciaries even though the lawyer does not render legal services in the transaction and is not governed by this Rule.

A lawyers' fund for client protection provides a means through the collective efforts of the bar to reimburse persons who have lost money or property as a result of dishonest conduct of a lawyer. Where such a fund has been established, a lawyer must participate where it is mandatory, and, even when it is voluntary, the lawyer should participate.

Keeping Impeccable Financial Records

The First rule: hire a competent CPA. The CPA is designed to keep books and records, not the attorney who is designed to argue.

MODEL RULES FOR CLIENT TRUST ACCOUNT RECORDS

Adopted by the American Bar Association

House of Delegates on August 9, 2010

RULE 1: RECORDKEEPING GENERALLY

A lawyer who practices in this jurisdiction shall maintain current financial records as provided in these Rules and required by [Rule 1.15 of the Model Rules of Professional Conduct], and shall retain the following records for a period of [five years] after termination of the representation:

> (a) receipt and disbursement journals containing a record of deposits to and withdrawals from client trust accounts, specifically identifying the date, source, and description of each item deposited, as well as the date, payee and purpose of each disbursement;

> (b) ledger records for all client trust accounts showing, for each separate trust client or beneficiary, the source of all funds deposited, the names of all persons for whom the funds are or were held, the amount of such funds, the descriptions and amounts of charges or withdrawals, and the names of all persons or entities to whom such funds were disbursed;

> (c) copies of retainer and compensation agreements with clients [as required by Rule 1.5 of the Model Rules of Professional Conduct];

> (d) copies of accountings to clients or third persons showing the disbursement of funds to them or on their behalf;

> (e) copies of bills for legal fees and expenses rendered to clients;

> (f) copies of records showing disbursements on behalf of clients;

> (g) the physical or electronic equivalents of all checkbook registers, bank statements, records of deposit, pre-numbered canceled checks, and substitute checks provided by a financial institution;

(h) records of all electronic transfers from client trust accounts, including the name of the person authorizing transfer, the date of transfer, the name of the recipient and confirmation from the financial institution of the trust account number from which money was withdrawn and the date and the time the transfer was completed;

(i) copies of [monthly] trial balances and [quarterly] reconciliations of the client trust accounts maintained by the lawyer; and

(j) copies of those portions of client files that are reasonably related to client trust account transactions.

Comment

Rule 1 enumerates the basic financial records that a lawyer must maintain with regard to all trust accounts of a law firm. These include the standard books of account, and the supporting records that are necessary to safeguard and account for the receipt and disbursement of client or third person funds as required by Rule 1.15 of the Model Rules of Professional Conduct or its equivalent. Consistent with Rule 1.15, this Rule proposes that lawyers maintain client trust account records for a period of five years after termination of each particular legal engagement or representation. Although these Model Rules address the accepted use of a client trust account by a lawyer when holding client or third person funds, some jurisdictions may permit a lawyer to deposit certain advance fees for legal services into the lawyer's business or operating account. In those situations, the lawyer should still be guided by the standards contained in these Model Rules.

Rule 1(g) requires that the physical or electronic equivalents of all checkbook registers, bank statements, records of deposit, pre-numbered canceled checks, and substitute checks be maintained for a period of five years after termination of each legal engagement or representation. The "Check Clearing for the 21st Century Act" or "Check 21 Act", codified at 12 U.S.C.§5001 *et. seq.*, recognizes "substitute checks" as the legal equivalent of an original check. A "substitute check" is defined at 12 U.S.C. §5002(16) as "paper reproduction of the original check that contains an image of the front and back of the original check; bears a magnetic ink character recognition ("MICR") line containing all the information appearing on the MICR line of the original check; conforms with generally applicable industry standards for substitute checks; and is suitable for automated processing in the same manner as the original check. Banks, as defined in 12 U.S.C. §5002(2), are not required to return to customers the original canceled checks. Most banks now provide electronic images of checks to customers who have access to their accounts on internet-based websites. It is the lawyer's responsibility to download electronic images. Electronic images shall be maintained for the requisite number of years and shall be readily available for printing upon request or shall be printed and maintained for the requisite number of years.

The ACH (Automated Clearing House) Network is an electronic funds transfer or payment system that primarily provides for the inter-bank clearing of electronic payments between originating and receiving participating financial institutions. ACH transactions are payment instructions to either debit or credit a deposit account. ACH payments are used in a variety of payment environments including bill payments, business-to-business payments, and government payments (e.g. tax refunds.) In addition to the primary use of ACH transactions, retailers and third parties use the ACH system for other types of transactions including electronic check conversion (ECC). ECC is the process of transmitting MICR information from the bottom of a check, converting check payments to ACH transactions depending upon the authorization given by the account holder at the point-of-purchase. In this type of transaction, the lawyer should be careful to comply with the requirements of Rule 1(h).

There are five types of check conversions where a lawyer should be careful to comply with the requirements of Rule 1(h). First, in a "point-of-purchase conversion," a paper check is converted into a debit at the point of purchase and the paper check is returned to the issuer. Second, in a "back-office conversion," a paper check is presented at the point of purchase and is later converted into a debit and the paper check is destroyed. Third, in an "account-receivable conversion," a paper check is converted into a debit and the paper check is destroyed. Fourth, in a "telephone-initiated debit" or "check-by-phone" conversion, bank account information is provided via the telephone and the information is converted to a debit. Fifth, in a "web-initiated debit," an electronic payment is initiated through a secure web environment. Rule 1(h) applies to each of the type of electronic funds transfers described. All electronic funds transfers shall be recorded and a lawyer should not re-use a check number which has been previously used in an electronic transfer transaction.

The potential of these records to serve as safeguards is realized only if the procedures set forth in Rule 1(i) are regularly performed. The trial balance is the sum of balances of each client's ledger card (or the electronic equivalent). Its value lies in comparing it on a monthly basis to a control balance. The control balance starts with the previous month's balance, then adds receipts from the Trust Receipts Journal and subtracts disbursements from the Trust Disbursements Journal. Once the total matches the trial balance, the reconciliation readily follows by adding amounts of any outstanding checks and subtracting any deposits not credited by the bank at month's end. This balance should agree with the bank statement. Quarterly reconciliation is recommended only as a minimum requirement; monthly reconciliation is the preferred practice given the difficulty of identifying an error (whether by the lawyer or the bank) among three months' transactions.

In some situations, documentation in addition to that listed in paragraphs (a) through (i) of Rule 1 is necessary for a complete understanding of a trust account transaction. The type of document that a lawyer must retain under paragraph (j) because it is "reasonably related" to a client trust transaction will vary depending on the nature of the transaction and the significance of the document in shedding light on the transaction. Examples of documents that typically must be retained under this paragraph include correspondence between the client and lawyer relating to a disagreement over fees or costs or the distribution of proceeds, settlement agreements contemplating payment of funds, settlement statements issued to the client, documentation relating to sharing litigation costs and attorney fees for subrogated claims, agreements for division of fees between lawyers, guarantees of payment to third parties out of proceeds recovered on behalf of a client, and copies of bills, receipts or correspondence related to any payments to third parties on behalf of a client (whether made from the client's funds or from the lawyer's funds advanced for the benefit of the client).

RULE 2: CLIENT TRUST ACCOUNT SAFEGUARDS

With respect to client trust accounts required by [Rule 1.15 of the Model Rules of Professional Conduct]:

> (a) only a lawyer admitted to practice law in this jurisdiction or a person under the direct supervision of the lawyer shall be an authorized signatory or authorize transfers from a client trust account;
>
> (b) receipts shall be deposited intact and records of deposit should be sufficiently detailed to identify each item; and

(c) withdrawals shall be made only by check payable to a named payee and not to cash, or by authorized electronic transfer.

Comment

Rule 2 enumerates minimal accounting controls for client trust accounts. It also enunciates the requirement that only a lawyer admitted to the practice of law in the jurisdiction or a person who is under the direct supervision of the lawyer shall be the authorized signatory or authorize electronic transfers from a client trust account. While it is permissible to grant limited nonlawyer access to a client trust account, such access should be limited and closely monitored by the lawyer. The lawyer has a non-delegable duty to protect and preserve the funds in a client trust account and can be disciplined for failure to supervise subordinates who misappropriate client funds. See, Rules 5.1 and 5.3 of the Model Rules of Professional Conduct.

Authorized electronic transfers shall be limited to (1) money required for payment to a client or third person on behalf of a client; (2) expenses properly incurred on behalf of a client, such as filing fees or payment to third persons for services rendered in connection with the representation; or (3) money transferred to the lawyer for fees that are earned in connection with the representation and are not in dispute; or (4) money transferred from one client trust account to another client trust account.

[3] The requirements in paragraph (b) that receipts shall be deposited intact mean that a lawyer cannot deposit one check or negotiable instrument into two or more accounts at the same time, a practice commonly known as a split deposit.

RULE 3: AVAILABILITY OF RECORDS

Records required by Rule 1 may be maintained by electronic, photographic, or other media provided that they otherwise comply with these Rules and that printed copies can be produced. These records shall be readily accessible to the lawyer.

Comment

Rule 3 allows the use of alternative media for the maintenance of client trust account records if printed copies of necessary reports can be produced. If trust records are computerized, a system of regular and frequent (preferably daily) back-up procedures is essential. If a lawyer uses third-party electronic or internet based file storage, the lawyer must make reasonable efforts to ensure that the company has in place, or will establish reasonable procedures to protect the confidentiality of client information. See, ABA Formal Ethics Opinion 398 (1995). Records required by Rule 1 shall be readily accessible and shall be readily available to be produced upon request by the client or third person who has an interest as provided in Model Rule 1.15, or by the official request of a disciplinary authority, including but not limited to, a subpoena duces tecum. Personally identifying information in records produced upon request by the client or third person or by disciplinary authority shall remain confidential and shall be disclosed only in a manner to ensure client confidentiality as otherwise required by law or court rule.

Rule 28 of the Model Rules for Lawyer Disciplinary Enforcement provides for the preservation of a lawyer's client trust account records in the event that the lawyer is transferred to disability inactive status, suspended, disbarred, disappears, or dies.

RULE 4: DISSOLUTION OF LAW FIRM

Upon dissolution of a law firm or of any legal professional corporation, the partners shall make reasonable arrangements for the maintenance of client trust account records specified in Rule 1.

Comment

Rules 4 and 5 provide for the preservation of a lawyer's client trust account records in the event of dissolution or sale of a law practice. Regardless of the arrangements the partners or shareholders make among themselves for maintenance of the client trust records, each partner may be held responsible for ensuring the availability of these records. For the purposes of these Rules, the terms "law firm," "partner," and "reasonable" are defined in accordance with Rules 1.0(c),(g), and (h) of the Model Rules of Professional Conduct

RULE 5: SALE OF LAW PRACTICE

Upon the sale of a law practice, the seller shall make reasonable arrangements for the maintenance of records specified in Rule 1.

The Model Rule on Financial Recordkeeping, adopted in February 1993, delineates the types of records that lawyers must maintain to satisfy the requirements in Rule 1.15 of the Model Rules of Professional Conduct. Specifically, Model Rule 1.15 requires a lawyer to preserve "complete records" with respect to a lawyer's client trust accounts and to "render a full accounting" for the receipt and distribution of trust property, but it does not include practical guidance to the lawyer on the maintenance of these records. The Model Rule on Financial Recordkeeping provided uniform and minimal standards for compliance with these fiduciary obligations and for establishing basic accounting control systems. See, Appendix A, attached.

Every United States jurisdiction has adopted the requirement of Model Rule 1.15 that a lawyer maintain "complete records." Twenty-eight jurisdictions have additional rules or comments outlining the types of records that must be maintained; an additional five jurisdictions direct lawyers to the ABA Model Rule on Financial Recordkeeping as a guide for recordkeeping requirements.

There have been many changes in banking laws and practices since the adoption of the Model Rule on Financial Recordkeeping. The Check Clearing for the 21st Century Act ("Check 21"), 12 U.S.C. §5001 et. seq., was adopted in 2003 and allows banks to use electronic images of checks as a substitute for canceled checks. In addition, many merchants now convert paper checks into electronic images and the original checks are often destroyed. Most jurisdictional rules, and the current ABA Model Rule on Financial Recordkeeping, require lawyers to maintain the original canceled checks. Accordingly, lawyers are inadvertently running afoul of their jurisdiction's rules of professional conduct. This resolution eliminates this danger for lawyers by defining what records a lawyer must maintain to satisfy the "complete records" requirement of Rule 1.15 and how those records must be maintained.

Along with changes to banking practices through "Check 21," methods of banking have changed for lawyers and their clients. Electronic banking, and specifically, wire transfers or electronic transfers of funds have become more prevalent. This form of banking presents a special set of problems for lawyers with trust accounts because there is often no discernible paper trail to the transaction. Records of these transactions can be found as part of the lawyer's monthly statement or through the lawyer's online banking system, but banks do not provide specific confirmation of electronic transactions as a matter of course. Lawyers must be proactive in securing the necessary records for these transactions.

This resolution addresses a lawyer's recordkeeping requirements following the electronic transfer of funds from client trust accounts and clarifies who can authorize transactions from client trust accounts. The resolution also addresses issues related to record maintenance and outlines necessary safeguards that a lawyer must have in place when using electronic record storage systems. Finally, the scope of the Model Rules for Client Trust Account Records has been clearly defined and the structure simplified.

Title and Structure

A goal of any ABA Model Rule is to serve as a guide to individual jurisdictions in attaining the highest standards in the practice of law. Model Rules should be clearly structured, focused, and provide easy to follow instructions to lawyers. The Model Rules are now organized into five separate Rules. This new organization increases the readability of the Model Rules and the associated comments.

The Model Rule on Financial Recordkeeping was adopted as a guideline for lawyers to follow in satisfying the "complete records" requirement of Model Rule 1.15 when the lawyer is handling the "property of clients or third persons." The requirements contained within the Model Rule were meant to primarily address the lawyer's handling of client trust accounts or money held in trust by the lawyer. The new Model Rules for Client Trust Account Records more accurately reflect the intended scope.

Rule 1: Recordkeeping Generally

New Rule 1 and its supporting comments address general recordkeeping requirements for all lawyers holding client funds. Many of the provisions remain unchanged from what was formerly Section A of the Model Rule on Financial Recordkeeping. The substantive changes to this section focus on advances in banking practices that have occurred since the Model Rule on Financial Recordkeeping was adopted.

"Check 21" was adopted to enable banks to process more checks electronically by allowing them to capture a picture of the front and back of a check along with the associated payment information and transmit that information electronically. This process eliminates the need for banks to move the actual paper check from bank to bank for processing because the captured image of the check becomes a "substitute check" and can be processed electronically. As a result of these electronic images, banks are now allowed to provide either the original canceled check or the "substitute check" to the account holder. Accordingly, the lawyer will either receive a canceled check, a "substitute check," or have access to an electronic image of the check through the bank's on-line system.

New Rule 1 specifically includes substitute checks as an alternative to pre-numbered canceled checks. The current Model Rule requires a lawyer to maintain the canceled check or its equivalent. Although a substitute check is legally the same as a canceled check, the addition of specific language eliminates the risk of disciplinary agencies finding a lawyer maintaining substitute checks in violation of the jurisdiction's rules.

The current Model Rule lacks any specific provisions for the maintenance of records following the electronic transfer of funds. While many individual jurisdictions have adopted provisions to cover the increase in electronic banking mechanisms, most jurisdictions still mirror the ABA Model Rule. New Rule 1 and its supporting comments seek to provide specific guidelines for securing the authorization for electronic transfers and for maintaining the necessary accounting information to satisfy the requirements of Model Rule 1.15.

New Rule 1 outlines the specific recordkeeping requirements for any electronic transfer of funds from a client trust account. Comments 3 and 4 delineate the many environments in which an electronic funds transfer or electronic check conversion can occur (e.g. wire transfers, electronic transfers of funds, and automatic clearing house (ACH) transactions). Electronic fund transfers are assumed to carry a greater risk of abuse than paper check withdrawals. Therefore, lawyers should maintain detailed information regarding each electronic transfer and be especially vigilant in complying with Rule 1(h).

Rule 2: Client Trust Account Safeguards

Rule 2 (formerly Section B) and its supporting comments address the minimum safeguards that must be in place with respect to client trust accounts. The vast majority of jurisdictions allow a nonlawyer employee to have access to and authorize transactions from a client trust account. While a lawyer should limit client trust account access and authorization, new Rule 2(a) allows an employee under the direct supervision of a lawyer to authorize transactions on a client trust account. Such authorization should be limited and the lawyer should closely monitor all transactions from client trust accounts. If a lawyer grants authorization privileges to nonlawyer employees, the lawyer remains personally and professionally liable for all transactions. See, Rule 5.1 (Responsibility of Partners, Managers, and Supervisory Lawyers) and Rule 5.3 (Responsibilities Regarding Non-lawyer Assistants) of the Model Rules of Professional Conduct.

Rule 3: Availability of Records

The lawyer's client trust account records may be maintained by electronic, photographic, computer or other media or in paper format at the lawyer's office or at an off-site storage facility. Regardless of which record storage option is chosen, the records must be readily accessible to the lawyer and the lawyer must be able to produce and print them upon request.

Many lawyers are now using third-party storage systems to store their files. Prior to using third-party or internet based file storage, the lawyer must ensure that the company has established reasonable procedures to protect client confidentiality and ensure that the files can be accessed by a disciplinary authority, client, or interested third-party, following issuance of a subpoena or other demand for production by a court.

Rule 28 of the Model Rules for Lawyer Disciplinary Enforcement provides for the preservation of a lawyer's client trust account records in the event that the lawyer is transferred to disability inactive status, suspended, disbarred, disappears, or dies.

Rule 4: Dissolution of Partnership and Rule 5: Sale of a Law Practice

It is the responsibility of all partners in a law firm to ensure the proper storage and accessibility of client trust account records. If a proper system is not established prior to the dissolution or sale of a law firm, each partner may be held personally and professionally responsible.

Conclusion

The Model Rules for Client Trust Account Records provide guidelines to lawyers for compliance with the "complete records" requirement of Rule 1.15 of the Model Rules of Professional Conduct by establishing minimum standards for maintaining a lawyer's financial records. The new Model Rules do not increase the regulatory obligation for lawyers. They seek to eliminate the risk of noncompliance by lawyers with client trust accounts in banks using "substitute checks" or electronic imaging of checks; to clarify the recordkeeping requirements for lawyers making electronic fund transfers; and to clarify record storage requirements. The new Model

Rules accommodate current standards of practice while continuing to protect the interests of clients.

Respectfully submitted,

Hon. Daniel J. Crothers, Chair

Standing Committee on Client Protection

August 2010

ABA MODEL RULE ON FINANCIAL RECORDKEEPING
ABA MODEL RULES FOR CLIENT TRUST ACCOUNT RECORDS

A. RULE 1. RECORDKEEPING GENERALLY

A lawyer who practices in this jurisdiction shall maintain current financial records as provided in this these Rules, and required by [Rule 1.15 of the Model Rules of Professional Conduct], and shall retain the following records for a period of [five years] after termination of the representation:

(1) (a). receipt and disbursement journals containing a record of deposits to and withdrawals from bank accounts which concern or affect the lawyer's practice of law, client trust accounts, specifically identifying the date, source, and description of each item deposited, as well as the date, payee and purpose of each disbursement;

(2) (b). ledger records for all client trust accounts required by [Rule 1.15 of the ABA Model Rules of Professional Conduct] showing, for each separate trust client or beneficiary, the source of all funds deposited, the names of all persons for whom the funds are or were held, the amount of such funds, the descriptions and amounts of charges or withdrawals, and the names of all persons or entities to whom such funds were disbursed;

(3) (c). copies of retainer and compensation agreements with clients [as required by Rule 1.5 of the Model Rules of Professional Conduct];

(4) (d). copies of accountings to clients or third persons showing the disbursement of funds to them or on their behalf;

(5) (e). copies of bills for legal fees and expenses rendered to clients;

(6) (f). copies of records showing disbursements on behalf of clients;

(7) (g). the physical or electronic equivalents of all checkbook registers, check stubs bank statements, records of deposit, pre-numbered canceled checks, and or their equivalent substitute checks provided by a financial institution;

(h). records of all electronic transfers from client trust accounts, including the name of the person authorizing transfer, the date of transfer, the name of the recipient and confirmation from the financial institution of the trust account number from which money was withdrawn and the date and the time the transfer was completed;

(8) (i). copies of [monthly] trial balances and [quarterly] reconciliations of the lawyer's client trust accounts maintained by the lawyer; and

(9) (j). copies of those portions of client files that are reasonably necessary for a complete understanding of the financial transactions pertaining to them related to client trust account transactions.

Comment

Paragraph A Rule 1 enumerates the basic financial records that a lawyer must maintain with regard to the business and all trust accounts of a law firm. These include the standard books of account, and the supporting records which are necessary to safeguard and account for the receipt and disbursement of client or third person funds as required by Rule 1.15 of the ABA Model Rules of Professional Conduct or its equivalent. Consistent with Rule 1.15, this rule proposes that lawyers maintain financial client trust account records and safekeeping records for a period of five years after termination of each particular legal engagement or representation. Although these Model Rules address the accepted use of a client trust account by a lawyer when holding client or third person funds, some jurisdictions may permit a lawyer to deposit certain advance fees for legal services into the lawyer's business or operating account. In those situations, the lawyer should still be guided by the standards contained in these Model Rules.

Rule 1(G) requires that the physical or electronic equivalents of all checkbook registers, bank statements, records of deposit, pre-numbered canceled checks, and substitute checks be maintained for a period of five years after termination of each legal engagement or representation. The "Check Clearing for the 21st Century Act" or "Check 21 Act", codified at 12 U.S.C.§5001 *et. seq.*, recognizes "substitute checks" as the legal equivalent of an original check.

A "substitute check" is defined at 12 U.S.C. §5002(16) as "paper reproduction of the original check that contains an image of the front and back of the original check; bears a magnetic ink character recognition ("MICR") line containing all the information appearing on the MICR line of the original check; conforms with generally applicable industry standards for substitute checks; and is suitable for automated processing in the same manner as the original check. Banks, as defined in 12 U.S.C. §5002(2), are not required to return to customers the original canceled checks. Most banks now provide electronic images of checks to customers who have access to their accounts on internet-based websites. It is the lawyer's responsibility to download electronic images. Electronic images shall be maintained for the requisite number of years and shall be readily available for printing upon request or shall be printed and maintained for the requisite number of years.

The ACH (Automated Clearing House) Network is an electronic funds transfer or payment system that primarily provides for the interbank clearing of electronic payments between originating and receiving participating financial institutions. ACH transactions are payment instructions to either debit or credit a deposit account. ACH payments are used in a variety of payment environments including bill payments, business-to-business payments, and government payments (e.g. tax refunds.) In addition to the primary use of ACH transactions, retailers and third parties use the ACH system for other types of transactions including electronic check conversion (ECC). ECC is the process of transmitting MICR information from the bottom of a check, converting check payments to ACH transactions depending upon the authorization given by the account holder at the point-of-purchase. In this type of transaction, the lawyer should be careful to comply with the requirements of Rule 1 (H).

There are five types of check conversions where a lawyer should be careful to comply with the requirements of Rule 1(H). First, in a "point-of-purchase conversion," a paper check is converted into a debit at the point of purchase and the paper check is returned to the issuer. Second, in a "back-office conversion," a paper check is presented at the point of purchase and is later converted into a debit and the paper check is destroyed. Third, in an "account-receivable conversion," a paper check is converted into a debit and the paper check is destroyed. Fourth, in a "telephone-initiated debit" or "check-by-phone" conversion, bank account information is provided via the telephone and the information is converted to a debit. Fifth, in a "web-initiated debit," an electronic payment is initiated through a secure web environment. Rule 1(H) applies to each of the type of electronic funds transfers described. All electronic funds transfers shall be recorded and a lawyer should be careful not to re-use a check number which has been previously used in an electronic transfer transaction.

The potential of these records to serve as safeguards is realized only if the procedures set forth in Paragraph A (8) Rule 1(i) are regularly performed. The trial balance is the sum of balances of each client's ledger card (or the computerized equivalent). Its value lies in comparing it on a monthly basis to a control balance. The control balance starts with the previous month's balance, then adds receipts from the Trust Receipts Journal and subtracts disbursements from the Trust Disbursements Journal. Once the total matches the trial balance, the reconciliation readily follows by adding amounts of any outstanding checks and subtracting any deposits not credited by the bank at month's end. This balance should agree with the bank statement. Quarterly reconciliation is recommended only as a minimum requirement; monthly reconciliation is the preferred practice given the difficulty of identifying an error (whether by the lawyer or the bank) among three months' transactions.

[6] In some situations, documentation in addition to that listed in paragraphs (a) through (i) of Rule 1 is necessary for a complete understanding of a trust account transaction. The type of document that a lawyer must retain under paragraph (j) because it is "reasonably related" to a client trust transaction will vary depending on the nature of the transaction and the significance of the document in shedding light on the transaction. Examples of documents that typically must be retained under this paragraph include correspondence between the client and lawyer relating to a disagreement over fees or costs or the distribution of proceeds, settlement agreements contemplating payment of funds, settlement statements issued to the client, documentation relating to sharing litigation costs and attorney fees for subrogated claims, agreements for division of fees between lawyers, guarantees of payment to third parties out of proceeds recovered on behalf of a client, and copies of bills, receipts or correspondence related to any payments to third parties on behalf of a client (whether made from the client's funds or from the lawyer's funds advanced for the benefit of the client).

RULE2. CLIENT TRUST ACCOUNT SAFEGUARDS

With respect to client trust accounts required by [Rule 1.15 of the ABA Model Rules of Professional Conduct]:

(1) A. only a lawyer admitted to practice law in this jurisdiction <u>or a person under the direct</u>
<u>supervision of the lawyer</u> shall be an authorized signatory on the account <u>or authorize</u>
<u>transfers from a client trust account</u>;

(2) <u>B.</u> receipts shall be deposited intact and records of deposit should be sufficiently detailed
to identify each item; and

(3) <u>C.</u> withdrawals shall be made only by check payable to a named payee and not to cash, or
by authorized bank <u>electronic</u> transfer.

Comment

<u>Paragraph B <u>Rule 2</u> enumerates minimal accounting controls for lawyer <u>client</u> trust accounts. It also enunciates the requirement that only a lawyer admitted to the practice of law in the jurisdiction <u>or a person who is under the direct supervision of the lawyer shall</u> be an the authorized signatory on a lawyer trust account <u>or authorize electronic transfers from a client trust account. While it is permissible to grant limited non-lawyer access to a client trust account, such access should be limited and closely monitored by the lawyer. The lawyer has a non-delegable duty to protect and preserve the funds in a client trust account and can be disciplined for failure to supervise subordinates who misappropriate client funds. See, Rule 5.1 and 5.3 of the Model Rules of Professional Conduct.</u>

<u>Authorized electronic transfers shall be limited to (1) money required for payment to a client or third person on behalf of a client; (2) expenses properly incurred on behalf of a client, such as filing fees or payment to third persons for services rendered in connection with the representation; or (3) money transferred to the lawyer for fees which are earned in connection with the representation and are not in dispute; or (4) money transferred from one client trust account to another client trust account.</u>

<u>The requirements in paragraph (b) that receipts shall be deposited intact mean that a lawyer cannot deposit one check or negotiable instrument into two or more accounts at the same time, a practice commonly known as a split deposit.</u>

C. <u>RULE 3. AVAILABILITY OF RECORDS</u>

Records required by this rule <u>Rule 1</u> may be maintained by electronic, photographic, computer or other media provided that they otherwise comply with this rule <u>these Rules</u> and provided further that printed copies can be produced. These Records shall be located at the lawyer's principal office in the jurisdiction or in a readily accessible location <u>readily accessible to the lawyer</u>.

Comment

Paragraph C <u>Rule 3</u> allows the use of alternative media for the maintenance of bookkeeping <u>client trust account</u> records if printed copies of necessary reports can be produced. If trust records are computerized, a system of regular and frequent (preferably daily) back-up procedures is essential. <u>If a lawyer uses third-party electronic or internet based file storage, the lawyer must make reasonable efforts to ensure that the company has in place, or will establish, reasonable procedures to protect the confidentiality of client information. See, ABA Formal Ethics Opinion 398 (1995). Records required by Rule 1 shall be readily accessible and shall be readily available to be produced upon request by the client or third person who has an interest as provided in Model Rule 1.15, or by the official request of a disciplinary authority, including but not limited to, a subpoena duces tecum. Personally identifying information in records produced upon request by the client or third person or by disciplinary authority shall remain confidential and shall be disclosed only in a manner to ensure client confidentiality as otherwise required by law or court rule</u>."

<u>Rule 28 of the Model Rules for Lawyer Disciplinary Enforcement provides for the preservation of a lawyer's client trust account records in the event that the lawyer is transferred to disability inactive status, suspended, disbarred, disappears, or dies.</u>

D. <u>RULE 4. DISSOLUTION OF LAW FIRM</u>

Upon dissolution of any partnership of lawyers <u>a law firm</u> or of any legal professional corporation, the partners or shareholders shall make appropriate <u>reasonable</u> arrangements for the maintenance of the <u>client trust account</u> records specified in Paragraph A of this Rule <u>Rule 1 of these rules</u>.

Comment

Paragraph D and E <u>Rules 4 and 5</u> provide for the preservation of a lawyer's client trust account records in the event of dissolution or sale of a law practice. <u>Regardless of the arrangements the partners or shareholders make among themselves for maintenance of the client trust records, each partner may be held responsible for ensuring the availability of these records.</u>

For the purposes of these Rules, the terms "law firm", "partner", and "reasonable" are defined in accordance with Rules 1.0 (c), (g), (h) of the Model Rules of Professional Conduct.

E. RULE 5. SALE OF LAW PRACTICE

Upon the sale of a law practice, the seller shall make appropriate reasonable arrangements for the maintenance of the records specified in Paragraph A of this Rule Rule 1 of these rules.

How to Write invoices that Clients will Pay

Collections are always a sensitive matter. The attorney needs to collect outstanding invoices, however does not want to disturb the client. One of the best ways is to add item 4 or interest to the bill.

1. Description of the work
2. Description of the amount of Time
3. Deliverables
4. Add interest

Fee Splitting

A division of a fee between lawyers who are not in the same firm may be made only if:

(1) the division is in proportion to the services performed by each lawyer or each lawyer assumes joint responsibility for the representation;

(2) the client agrees to the arrangement, including the share each lawyer will receive, and the agreement is confirmed in writing; and

(3) the total fee is reasonable.

Division of Fee

A division of fee is a single billing to a client covering the fee of two or more lawyers who are not in the same firm. A division of fee facilitates association of more than one lawyer in a matter in which neither alone could serve the client as well, and most often is used when the fee is contingent and the division is between a referring lawyer and a trial specialist. Paragraph (e) permits the lawyers to divide a fee either on the basis of the proportion of services they render or if each lawyer assumes responsibility for the representation as a whole. In addition, the client must agree to the arrangement, including the share that each lawyer is to receive, and the agreement must be confirmed in writing. Contingent fee agreements must be in a writing signed by the client and must otherwise comply with paragraph (c) of this Rule. Joint responsibility for the representation entails financial and ethical responsibility for the representation as if the lawyers were associated in a partnership. A lawyer should only refer a matter to a lawyer whom the referring lawyer reasonably believes is competent to handle the matter. See Rule 1.1.

Paragraph (e) does not prohibit or regulate division of fees to be received in the future for work done when lawyers were previously associated in a law firm.

Resolving Fee Disputes

Disputes over Fees

If a procedure has been established for resolution of fee disputes, such as an arbitration or mediation procedure established by the bar, the lawyer must comply with the procedure when it is mandatory, and, even when it is voluntary, the lawyer should conscientiously consider submitting to it. Law may prescribe a procedure for determining a lawyer's fee, for example, in representation of an executor or administrator, a class or a person entitled to a reasonable fee as part of the measure of damages. The lawyer entitled to such a fee and a lawyer representing another party concerned with the fee should comply with the prescribed procedure.

How Long Do I keep the Closed Case File?

Duty to maintain client files and property-

Questions also arise as to how long the lawyer who assumes responsibility for the deceased lawyer's client files should keep the files for those clients he or she is unable to locate. ABA Informal Opinion 1384 (1977) provides general guidance in this area. We believe that the principles set out in that opinion are applicable to the instant question. Informal Opinion 1384 states as follows:

A lawyer does not have a general duty to preserve all of his files permanently. Mounting and substantial storage costs can affect the cost of legal services, and the public interest is not served by unnecessary and avoidable additions to the cost of legal services.

But clients (and former clients) reasonably expect from their lawyers that valuable and useful information in the lawyers' files, and not otherwise readily available to the clients, will not be prematurely and carelessly destroyed to the clients' detriment.

Informal Opinion 1384 then lists eight guidelines that lawyers should follow when deciding whether to discard old client files. One of these guidelines states that a lawyer should not "destroy or discard items that clearly or probably belong to the client. Such items include those furnished to the lawyer by or in behalf of the client, and original documents." Another suggests that a lawyer should not "destroy or discard information that the lawyer knows or should know may still be necessary or useful in the assertion or defense of the client's position in a matter for which the applicable statutory limitations period has not expired."

There is no simple answer to this question. Each file must be evaluated separately. Reasonable efforts must be made to contact the clients and inform them that their lawyer has died, such as mailing letters to the last known address of the clients explaining that their lawyer has died and requesting instructions. [FN15]

Finally, questions arise with regard to unclaimed funds in the deceased lawyer's client trust account. In this situation, reasonable efforts must be made to contact the clients. If this fails, then the lawyer should maintain the funds in the trust account. Whether the lawyer should follow the procedures as outlined in the applicable Disposition of Unclaimed Property Act that is in effect in the lawyer's state jurisdiction is a question of law that this Committee cannot address. [FN16]

FN1. See Model Rule of Professional Conduct 1.16 ("... a lawyer shall not represent a client or, where representation has commenced, shall withdraw from the representation of the client if: ... (2) the lawyer's physical or mental condition materially impairs the lawyer's ability to represent the client....")

FN2. See Murphy v. Riggs, > 213 N.W. 110 (Mich.1927) (fiduciary obligations of loyalty and confidentiality continue after agency relationship concluded); Eoff v. Irvine, > 18 S.W. 907 (Mo.1892) (same.)

FN3. See Vollgraff v. Block, > 458 N.Y.S.2d 437.

Additional articles on this topic include:

1) "File Retention Policies and Requirements" Kenneth L. Jorgensen, 61-DEC Bench & B. Minn. 12 (2004)

2) "Ask ETHICSearch", Peter Geraghty 12 NO. 2 Prof. Law. 24 (2001) (ethical obligations of lawyers to safeguard client files in the event of the merger or dissolution of law firm)

3) "Focus on Professional Responsibility--Ownership of Lawyer's Files About Client Representations; Who Gets the 'Original'? Who Pays for Copies?" John W. Allen, 79 Michigan Bar Journal 1062-65 (2000).

4) "Who Owns the File--The Attorney or the Client?" 7 Law Office Administrator 6-7 (August 1998).

5) "Client Files: Handle with Care," Pamela Phillips and Merri A. Baldwin, 18 California Lawyer 66-68 (May 1998).

6) "How Long Should You Retain Client Files?" 83 Illinois Bar Journal 649-50 (1995).

7) "Ethical Considerations in the Retention of Law Firm Client Files," John C. Montana, 1 The ISG Update 5-7 (June 1999).

State Rule Variations

Of the states that have adopted new rules since the ABA's adoption of the Model Rules, the following have made significant changes in the recordkeeping requirements of Rule 1.15(a) or have specifically modified the rule's suggested time period for preserving records of account funds and property:

Alabama, Alaska, Colorado, Florida, Georgia, North Dakota, and South Carolina have a six-year records retention period.

Illinois, Mississippi, and Nevada use a 7-year records retention period.

Connecticut defers to applicable law as to the length of the retention period.

New Hampshire's rule incorporates the New Hampshire Supreme Court's rules with respect to required recordkeeping, and uses a retention period of six years after final distribution, rather than measuring the period from the date of the conclusion of the representation.

New Jersey uses a records retention period of seven years after the event recorded, rather than measuring the period from the date of the conclusion of the representation.

New York specifies seven kinds of records that must be maintained, and uses a seven-year retention period. Production of records is required in certain enumerated circumstances, specifying that all books and records so produced shall be kept confidential, and members of dissolving firms are directed to make arrangements for maintaining the required records.

Wisconsin uses a six-year record retention period, and specifies six classes of required records. The records must be submitted to the Board of Attorneys Professional Responsibility at its request or upon direction of the state supreme court.

WHAT MUST BE DONE WHEN A CLIENT ENTERS OR LEAVES THE FIRM

Rule 1.14(d) provides:

"The lawyer may retain papers relating to the client to the extent permitted by law."

There may be portions of the client's file that are not necessary for preserving the client's interests and to which the client is not entitled. It is beyond the scope of this opinion to delineate the limits of Rule 1.14(d). The authorities are not consistent on this issue. *See Corrigan v. Armstrong,* 824 S.W.2d 92 (Mo. App. 1992); Kansas Bar Assoc. Op. 92-05 (July 30, 1992); Connecticut Bar Assoc. Op. 92-21 (July 22, 1992); California State Bar Op. 1992-127, Oregon State Bar Op. 1991-125 (July 1991); Vermont Bar Assoc. Op. 91-3. At least one court has found that the actions of a departing attorney who sent form dismissal agreements urging his previous clients to terminate their arrangements with the former law firm were an "intentional interference with performance of contract by a third person." *Adler, Barish, Daniels, Levin and Creskoff v. Epstein,* 482 Pa. 416, 393 A.2d 1175 (1978). But see id., dissenting opinion, which concludes that the direct solicitation by the departing lawyer had Constitutional protection and was not illegal or unethical. *See also* ABA/BNA Manual of Professional Conduct 91:706-710; Charles C. Marvel, *Annotation, Rights of Attorneys Leaving Firm with Respect to Firm Clients,* 1 A.L.R.4th 1164 (1980). *See Corti,* 417 N.E.2d at 768 (rejecting an agreement under which a law firm performed all legal services on certain matters but was required to turn over all fees received on these matters to a former member of the firm); *Champion v. Superior Court (Boccardo),* 247 Cal. Rptr. 624 (1988) (California law partnership agreement, under which firm was entitled to receive from withdrawing partner almost all fees he would earn from work performed for partnership's clients, violates "unconscionable fee" provision of DR 2-107 and public policy); *see* generally ABA/BNA Manual of Professional Conduct 91:710-12.

Electronic Communication Challenges

Every written, recorded or electronic communication from a lawyer soliciting professional employment from a prospective client known to be in need of legal services in a particular matter shall include the words "Advertising Material" on the outside envelope, if any, and at the beginning and ending of any recorded or electronic communication, unless the recipient of the communication is a person specified in paragraphs (a) (1) or (a) (2).

The requirement in Rule 7.3(c) that certain communications be marked "Advertising Material" does not apply to communications sent in response to requests of potential clients or their spokespersons or sponsors. General announcements by lawyers, including changes in personnel or office location, do not constitute communications soliciting professional employment from a client known to be in need of legal services within the meaning of this Rule.

The basic rule of electronic communication-every e-mail can and will be used against you in a court of law-even the e-mails of your staff!

Can an Attorney Secretly Record Conversations?

The ABA in late 2001 reversed its original opinion and held that recording is ethical. *See* ABA Formal Eth. Op. 01-422 (2001). The opinion holds that "the mere act of secretly but lawfully recording a conversation inherently is not deceitful." But, it goes on to say that many states have substantive law making it a crime to record without consent of all parties, and, as noted below, many states disagree with the ABA's opinion. The committee split on whether a lawyer could record his own client without consent. Go figure. *See also Anderson v. Hale*, __ F.Supp.2d__ (N.D. Ill. No. 00 c 2021 Apr. 23, 2001) (work product protection destroyed over tapes surreptitiously recorded with witnesses since "people who speak to attorneys in civil cases reasonably expect that they are not being recorded.")

UNITED STATES COURT OF APPEALS

FOR THE SECOND CIRCUIT

August Term, 2009

(Argued: April 19, 2010 Decided: August 13, 2010)

Docket No. 09-3685-cv

MARSHALL CARO,

Plaintiff-Appellant,

–v.–

ERIC WEINTRAUB, DAVID H. WEINTRAUB, GLENN WILLIAM DOWD, AND DAY PITNEY LLP,

Defendants-Appellees.

Before:

CABRANES, WESLEY, LIVINGSTON, *Circuit Judges.*

Appeal from an order of the United States District Court for the District of Connecticut (Dorsey, *J.*), entered on August 4, 2009, dismissing appellant Marshall Caro's complaint.

AFFIRMED.

MARSHALL CARO, *pro se*, Greenwich, CT, *for Plaintiff-*

Appellant.

N ALLA B. TAYLOR, Day Pitney LLP, Hartford, CT (Erik
H. Beard, *on the brief*), *for Defendants-
Appellees Dowd and Day Pitney LLP.*

WESLEY *Circuit Judge*:

Plaintiff-Appellant Marshall Caro filed a complaint in the United States District Court for the District
of Connecticut (Dorsey, *J.*) alleging, *inter alia*, a civil cause of action under Title III of the Omnibus
Crime Control and Safe Streets Act of 1968, codified at 18 U.S.C. §§ 2510-21 ("Title III" or the
"Wiretap Act"). The district court dismissed Caro's complaint. We affirm, and, in so doing, hold that
the exception to the one-party consent provision of 18 U.S.C. § 2511(2)(d) requires that a
communication be intercepted for the purpose of a tortuous or criminal act that is independent of the
intentional act of recording.

I. BACKGROUND

In early February 2008, Elizabeth Caro, who was in the final days of a painful battle with lung cancer,
was visited by her sons Eric and David Weintraub, along with their families, and her brother and sister-
in-law Thomas and Lynn Corrigan. During the visit, Elizabeth spoke with her sister-in-law, Lynn, in
the kitchen about Lynn's desire to David used a program called "Recorder," which allowed his iPhone
to operate as a recording device… have Elizabeth sign a draft of a will that Thomas had prepared. The
draft named Thomas as the executor of Elizabeth's estate and contained provisions to which Elizabeth
allegedly objected. Elizabeth's husband, Marshall Caro — the plaintiff-appellant here — informed
Lynn that he had already hired an attorney to prepare their wills and that in their meeting with their
attorney, Elizabeth had expressed different intentions than those set out in Thomas's draft. At some
point during this conversation, David and Eric Weintraub entered the kitchen. David placed his iPhone
on the kitchen table and, unbeknownst to Marshall, used the device to record the conversation. After
the recording began, Thomas also entered the kitchen. It appears from Caro's complaint that the
conversation at times included Thomas Corrigan and David Weintraub and, in the end, became quite
heated between those involved. Four days later, on February 6, 2008, Elizabeth died without

completing a will. Marshall filed Elizabeth's death certificate with the Connecticut Probate Court and filed a Petition for Letters of Administration for Elizabeth's estate. Eric and David Weintraub, represented by attorneys from Day Pitney LLP, filed an Opposition to Marshall Caro's petition. The Probate Court held a hearing on April 21, 2008. David testified that he had recordings of the kitchen conversation between Marshall and Elizabeth, and his attorney submitted a CD of the recordings. On February 27, 2009, Marshall Caro filed a complaint in the United States District Court for the District of Connecticut (Dorsey, *J.*), alleging violations of Title III, along with various Connecticut state law claims. In addition to David and Eric Weintraub, Caro named as defendants Day Pitney LLP and one of its lawyers, Glenn William Dowd. Upon Day Pitney's motion and over Caro's objection, the district court relieved Day Pitney from Eric and David Weintraub filed *pro se* motions to dismiss that adopted by reference Day Pitney's arguments. Connecticut's Local Civil Rule 83.13 and allowed a firm attorney to represent Day Pitney for the purpose of filing a motion to dismiss the complaint4 Defendants moved to dismiss, arguing, *inter alia*, that the recorded conversations did not qualify as "oral communications" within the scope of Title III because David Weintraub was a party to the conversation and Caro had no reasonable expectation of privacy in the conversation. Caro opposed the motion, arguing that he did not reasonably expect to be recorded and that David was not a party to the conversation. He also requested leave to amend his complaint. The district court granted the motion to dismiss and denied Caro's motion to amend his complaint. *Caro v.*15 *Weintraub*, No. 3:09 CV 00335, 2009 WL 2358919, at 1 (D. Conn. July 31, 2009). The district court agreed that the recordings were not "oral communications" under the Wiretap Act because David Weintraub was a party to the conversation and Caro did not have a reasonable expectation that his conversation was private. *Id*. at 2-3. The district court declined to exercise supplemental jurisdiction over Caro's state law claims. *Id*. At 3 Caro appealed.

II. DISCUSSION

We review the dismissal of a complaint *de novo*, accepting all factual allegations in the complaint as true and drawing all reasonable inferences in favor of the plaintiff. *Chambers v. Time Warner, Inc.*, 282 F.3d 147, 152 (2d Cir. 2002). To survive a motion to dismiss, the complaint must plead sufficient facts to make out a plausible claim to relief. *Bell Atl. Corp. v. Twombly*, 550 U.S. 544, 570 (2007). When, as here, the complaint is filed by a *pro se* plaintiff, we construe the complaint liberally, interpreting it "to raise the strongest arguments that [it] *suggest[s]*." *Triestman v. Fed. Bureau of*

Prisons, 470 F.3d 471, 474 (2d Cir. 2006) (per curiam); *accord Harris v. Mills*, 572 F.3d 66, 72 (2d Cir. 2009). In relevant part, the Wiretap Act affords a civil cause of action to an aggrieved individual who has had her oral communications intentionally intercepted by a party to those communications for the purpose of committing a crime or tort. 18 U.S.C. §§ 2520, 2511(1), 2511(2) (d). We hold that David Weintraub was a party to the conversation, but Caro did not allege a tort that could provide the independent tortuous intent necessary to bring a civil claim under the Wiretap Act. Thus, it is futile to allow him to amend his complaint.

A. Party to the Conversation

The district court found that David Weintraub was a party to the relevant conversation, and we agree. Caro argues that David Weintraub was not a party to the conversation because there were actually multiple conversations that occurred in the kitchen, and the participants in the conversations did not invite David to join any of them. Limiting ourselves, as we must, to the facts pled in the complaint, we conclude that David Weintraub was a party to the conversation for purposes of the Wiretap Act. In the context of the statute, a party to the conversation is one who takes part in the conversation. Caro offers — and we can find — no support for the proposition that one must be invited to a conversation in order to be a party to it. Caro admits in his complaint that David Weintraub was present at the table during the conversation in the kitchen and that David "spoke up a few times urging [Caro] to continue." Those facts are sufficient to establish that David was a party to the conversation. Concluding that David Weintraub was a party to the conversation is not fatal to Caro's claims. The Wiretap Act forbids someone who is a party to a conversation to record it, if the "oral . . . communication is intercepted for the purpose of committing any criminal or tortious act." 10 U.S.C. § 2511(2) (d). Invocation of this provision raises the question of what must be alleged to demonstrate tortuous intent.

B. Tortuous Intent

The statute requires that an oral communication be intercepted "for the purpose of committing any criminal or tortious act." 18 U.S.C. § 2511(2) (d). The district court did not address this issue and the original complaint as filed does not allege a tortuous intent behind David Weintraub's recording. Caro requested leave before the Under the version of Federal Rule of Civil Procedure 15(a) in effect on May 28, 2009, the date of Caro's Opposition to the Motion to Dismiss, Caro had the right to amend his complaint "once as a matter of course . . . before being served with a responsive pleading." Fed. R. Civ.

P.15 (a) (1) (amended 2009)…. In *Desnick v. American Broadcasting Cos.*, 44 F.3d 1345, 1347-48 (7th Cir. 1995), a producer of the ABC show *PrimeTime Live* arranged for individuals posing as patients to enter the Desnick Eye Center and to film their encounters using concealed cameras. *PrimeTime Live* eventually aired a segment on its "undercover investigation," asserting misconduct by Center employees. *Id.* at 1348. Center employees brought suit, charging in part that ABC had used an illegal wiretap under Title III. *Id.* at 1353.

The Seventh Circuit upheld the dismissal of the employees' Wiretap Act claims, concluding that ABC did not send the "patients" into the Center in order to commit a crime, tort, or other injurious act. *Id.* Even if the *PrimeTime Live* episode that followed the taping was defamatory, there was no evidence that ABC sent the test patients into the Center for the purpose of defaming the Center employees. *Id.* In *Sussman v. American Broadcasting Cos.*, 186 F.3d 13 1200, 1201 (9th Cir. 1999), ABC conducted an undercover investigation of the Psychic Marketing Group using various surveillance devices; two employees of the Group brought suit. The employees did not allege "that the tape was made for the purpose of committing some other subsequent crime or tort," but instead "argue[d] that the taping *itself* was tortuous." *Id.* at 1202. The Ninth Circuit found that this allegation was insufficient to meet the requirements of the1 statute. "Where the taping is legal, but is done for the purpose of facilitating some further impropriety, such as blackmail, § 2511 [of Title III] applies. Where the *purpose* is not illegal or tortuous, but the means are, the victims must seek redress elsewhere." *Id.* at 1202-03 (emphasis added); *accord Lucas v. Fox News Network, LLC*, 248 F.3d 1180, 2001 WL 100181, at *4 (11th Cir. Jan. 16, 2001) (per curiam); *Vazquez-Santos v. El Mundo Broad. Corp.*, 219 F. Supp. 2d 221, 229-30 (D.P.R. 2002).

The legislative history of the Wiretap Act is also instructive. The Wiretap Act as initially proposed did not prohibit interception where one of the parties to the communication consented, regardless of the parties' intent. *See* S. Rep. No. 90-1097, at 2182 (1968). Senator Philip A. Hart objected to the broad language, observing that it permitted "surreptitious monitoring of a conversation by a party to the conversation, even though the monitoring may be for insidious purposes such as blackmail, stealing business secrets, or other criminal or tortious acts in violation of Federal or State laws." *Id.* at 2236. Senator Hart and9 Senator John L. McClellan proposed an amendment to the bill that would limit the one-party consent rule to "private persons who act in a defensive fashion." 114 Cong. Rec.14694 (1968). This meant that interceptions by a party to the conversation would be forbidden if they were made "with an unlawful motive," such as "blackmailing the other party, threatening him, or publicly embarrassing him." *Id.* However, a party to a criminal conversation that recorded the conversation in order to bring evidence to the police or recording "out of a legitimate desire to protect himself and his own conversations from later distortions or other unlawful or injurious uses by the other party" would be protected under the statute. *Id.* The amendment passed. *Id.* at 14695. As the Eighth Circuit so aptly observed, it is "apparent from the context in which [Title III] was enacted that the sort of conduct contemplated was an interception by a party to a conversation with an intent to use that interception against the non-consenting party in some harmful way and in a manner in which the offending party had no right to proceed." *Meredith v. Gavin*, 446 F.2d17 794, 799 (8th Cir. 1971).

There is a temporal thread that runs through the fabric of the statute and the case law. At the time of the recording the offender must intend to use the recording to commit a criminal or tortuous act. Merely intending to record the plaintiff is not enough. If, at the moment he hits "record," the offender does not intend to use the recording for criminal or tortuous purposes, there is no violation. But if, at the time of the recording, the offender plans to use the recording to harm the other party to the conversation, a civil cause of action exists under the Wiretap Act. Intent may not be inferred simply by demonstrating that the intentional act of recording itself constituted a tort. A simultaneous tort arising from the act of recording itself is insufficient. Congress chose the word "purpose" for a reason. Therefore, the offender must have as her objective a tortuous or criminal result. Had Congress intended for the act of recording itself to provide the tortuous intent necessary, it could have chosen to define the exception in terms of interception of oral communications *resulting in* a tortuous or criminal act. But Congress limited the cause of action to instances where one party to the conversation deliberately seeks to harm the other participant through the information intercepted.

We join the courts that have considered this question, and hold that a cause of action under § 2511(2)(d) requires that the interceptor intends to commit a crime or tort independent of the act of recording itself. Thus, to survive a motion to dismiss, a plaintiff must plead sufficient facts to support an inference that the offender intercepted the communication for the purpose of a tortuous or criminal act that is independent of the intentional act of recording. The only tort Caro asserts in his complaint that could plausibly provide the intent necessary to bring the recording under the Wiretap Act is invasion of privacy, a tort recognized under Connecticut common law. *See Goodrich v. Waterbury Republican-Am., Inc.*, 188 Conn. 107, 127-28 (1982). Other circuits appear to have implicitly recognized invasion of privacy as a tort that could provide the necessary intent to bring a recording within the purview of the Wiretap Act. *See, e.g., Deteresa v. Am. Broad. Cos.*, 121 F.3d 460, 467 n.4 (9th Cir. 1997); *Phillips v. Bell*, No. 08-1420, 2010 WL 517629, at 7 (10th Cir. Feb. 12, 2010). But, under Connecticut law, invasion of privacy includes four distinct types of incursion that "otherwise have almost nothing in common except that each represents an interference with the right of the plaintiff to be let alone." *Goodrich*, 188 Conn. at 127-28 (quoting Prosser, *Torts* (4th ed. 1971) § 117, p. 804) (quotation marks omitted). The four categories of invasion of privacy are:

"(a) unreasonable intrusion upon the seclusion of another; (b) appropriation of the other's name or likeness; (c) unreasonable publicity given to the other's private life; or (d) publicity that unreasonably places the other in a false light before the public." *Id.* at 128.

Caro specifically pled invasion of privacy by unreasonable intrusion upon the seclusion of another, as opposed to a general claim of invasion of privacy. Connecticut courts have interpreted this version of the tort as the intentional invasion "upon the solitude or seclusion of another or his private affairs or concerns . . . if the intrusion would be highly offensive to a reasonable person."15 *Bonanno v. Dan Perkins Chevrolet*, No. CV 99-066602, 2000 WL16 192182, (Conn. Super. Ct. Feb. 4, 2000) (quoting 317 Restatement (Second) of Torts, § 652B (1977)); *accord Birge*18 *v. Med. Elec. Distribs., Inc.*, No. 075000540, 2009 WL 1959393 (Conn. Super. Ct. June 5, 2009); *Hellanbrand v. Nat'l Waste Assocs., LLC*, No. CV 075010727, 2008 WL 442136 (Conn. Super. Ct. Jan. 31, 2008).

The Restatement (Second) of Torts is valuable to our analysis as the Connecticut Supreme Court often embraces it when confronting an invasion of privacy claim. *See, e.g., Foncello v. Amorossi*, 284 Conn. 225, 234 (2007); *Goodrich*, 188 Conn. at 128.

Invasion of privacy through intrusion upon seclusion presents a problem for Caro — it is a tort that occurs through the act of interception itself. "The intrusion itself makes the defendant subject to liability, even though there is no publication or other use of any kind of the information outlined." Restatement (Second) of Torts § 652B (1977). Nothing more is required after the interception is made for liability to attach based on this tort. All that is required is that the tortfeasor intended to commit the act that was the basis for the invasion — as Caro alleges here, setting up the iPhone and hitting "record." The remaining three categories of invasion of privacy cannot be accomplished simply by intercepting one's communications; the tortfeasor is required to take an affirmative step or steps beyond the recording or the nature of the tort is such that interception would not further it. *See Gleason v. Smolinski*, No. NNH CV 065005107S, 2009 WL 2506607 (Conn. Super. Ct. July 20, 2009)

At first glance, the legislative history suggests that invasion of privacy was a tort Congress intended to reach in the Wiretap Act. When Senator Hart proposed the amendment that forbade interception when one party to the conversation operated with tortious or criminal intent, he noted that the blanket one-party consent rule left "wide open the problem of . . . many . . . abuses of the right of privacy." 114 Cong. Rec. 14694 (1968). However, he then went on to distinguish the injuries he wished to avoid through the amendment — "blackmailing the other party, threatening him, or publicly embarrassing him" — from "legitimate" uses like protection from "later distortions or other unlawful or injurious uses by the other party." *Id.*

It was not invasion of the right of privacy *per se* that Senator Hart wished to avoid through his proposal, but invasions and abuses that would result through use of the interception itself. The language and history of the Wiretap Act indicate that Congress authored the exception to the one-party consent rule to prevent abuses stemming from *use* of the recording not the mere *act* of recording. Connecticut's tort of invasion of privacy by intrusion upon the seclusion of another occurs through the simple act of the recording *itself* and therefore cannot satisfy the Wiretap Act's requirement of a separate and independent tortuous intent. Based on the facts alleged in Caro's complaint, intrusion upon the seclusion of another is the only category of invasion of privacy that could have possibly transpired here and Caro did not tell us or the district court if he has another tort in mind. Even if Caro were granted leave to amend his complaint and given the opportunity to allege that Weintraub had the intent to invade his privacy, that intent could only apply to invasion of privacy by intrusion upon the seclusion of another, which we hold cannot serve as the basis for the statutorily required tortuous intent.

Thus, we need not reach the question of whether any of the other three categories of invasion of privacy could serve as a predicate to the necessary intent. We need only say here that to bring a claim under the Wiretap Act, the offender must intercept with tortuous intent that relates to a tort independent from the act of recording itself, and invasion of privacy by intrusion on the seclusion of another cannot serve that purpose. Because Caro does not allege an independent tort that could provide the basis for the tortuous intent necessary to bring a claim under the Wiretap Act, allowing him leave to amend his complaint would be futile.

Conclusion

For the foregoing reasons, the district court's order of August 4, 2009, dismissing Caro's complaint, is hereby AFFIRMED.

UNAUTHORIZED PRACTICE OF LAW
UPL

Unauthorized Practice of Law; Multijurisdictional Practice of Law

(a) A lawyer shall not practice law in a jurisdiction in violation of the regulation of the legal profession in that jurisdiction, or assist another in doing so.

(b) A lawyer who is not admitted to practice in this jurisdiction shall not:

(1) except as authorized by these Rules or other law, establish an office or other systematic and continuous presence in this jurisdiction for the practice of law; or

(2) hold out to the public or otherwise represent that the lawyer is admitted to practice law in this jurisdiction.

(c) A lawyer admitted in another United States jurisdiction, and not disbarred or suspended from practice in any jurisdiction, may provide legal services on a temporary basis in this jurisdiction that:

(1) are undertaken in association with a lawyer who is admitted to practice in this jurisdiction and who actively participates in the matter;

(2) are in or reasonably related to a pending or potential proceeding before a tribunal in this or another jurisdiction, if the lawyer, or a person the lawyer is assisting, is authorized by law or order to appear in such proceeding or reasonably expects to be so authorized;

(3) are in or reasonably related to a pending or potential arbitration, mediation, or other alternative dispute resolution proceeding in this or another jurisdiction, if the services arise out of or are reasonably related to the lawyer's practice in a jurisdiction in which the lawyer is admitted to practice and are not services for which the forum requires pro hac vice admission; or

(4) are not within paragraphs (c) (2) or (c) (3) and arise out of or are reasonably related to the lawyer's practice in a jurisdiction in which the lawyer is admitted to practice.

(d) A lawyer admitted in another United States jurisdiction, and not disbarred or suspended from practice in any jurisdiction, may provide legal services in this jurisdiction that:

(1) are provided to the lawyer's employer or its organizational affiliates and are not services for which the forum requires pro hac vice admission; or

(2) are services that the lawyer is authorized to provide by federal law or other law of this jurisdiction.

Rule 5.5 Unauthorized Practice of Law; Multijurisdictional Practice of Law - Comment

A lawyer may practice law only in a jurisdiction in which the lawyer is authorized to practice. A lawyer may be admitted to practice law in a jurisdiction on a regular basis or may be authorized by court rule or order or by law to practice for a limited purpose or on a restricted basis. Paragraph (a) applies to unauthorized practice of law by a lawyer, whether through the lawyer's direct action or by the lawyer assisting another person.

The definition of the practice of law is established by law and varies from one jurisdiction to another. Whatever the definition, limiting the practice of law to members of the bar protects the public against rendition of legal services by unqualified persons. This Rule does not prohibit a lawyer from employing the services of paraprofessionals and delegating functions to them, so long as the lawyer supervises the delegated work and retains responsibility for their work. See Rule 5.3.

A lawyer may provide professional advice and instruction to nonlawyers whose employment requires knowledge of the law; for example, claims adjusters, employees of financial or commercial institutions, social workers, accountants and persons employed in government agencies. Lawyers also may assist independent nonlawyers, such as paraprofessionals, who are authorized by the law of a jurisdiction to provide particular law-related services. In addition, a lawyer may counsel nonlawyers who wish to proceed pro se.

Other than as authorized by law or this Rule, a lawyer who is not admitted to practice generally in this jurisdiction violates paragraph (b) if the lawyer establishes an office or other systematic and continuous presence in this jurisdiction for the practice of law. Presence may be systematic and continuous even if the lawyer is not physically present here. Such a lawyer must not hold out to the public or otherwise represent that the lawyer is admitted to practice law in this jurisdiction. See also Rules 7.1(a) and 7.5(b).

There are occasions in which a lawyer admitted to practice in another United States jurisdiction, and not disbarred or suspended from practice in any jurisdiction, may provide legal services on a temporary basis in this jurisdiction under circumstances that do not create an unreasonable risk to the interests of their clients, the public or the courts. Paragraph (c) identifies four such circumstances. The fact that conduct is not so identified does not imply that the conduct is or is not authorized. With the exception of paragraphs (d) (1) and (d) (2), this Rule does not authorize a lawyer to establish an office or other systematic and continuous presence in this jurisdiction without being admitted to practice generally here.

There is no single test to determine whether a lawyer's services are provided on a "temporary basis" in this jurisdiction, and may therefore be permissible under paragraph (c). Services may be "temporary" even though the lawyer provides services in this jurisdiction on a recurring basis, or for an extended period of time, as when the lawyer is representing a client in a single lengthy negotiation or litigation.

Paragraphs (c) and (d) apply to lawyers who are admitted to practice law in any United States jurisdiction, which includes the District of Columbia and any state, territory or commonwealth of the United States. The word "admitted" in paragraph (c) contemplates that the lawyer is authorized to practice in the jurisdiction in which the lawyer is admitted and excludes a lawyer who while technically admitted is not authorized to practice, because, for example, the lawyer is on inactive status.

Paragraph (c)(1) recognizes that the interests of clients and the public are protected if a lawyer admitted only in another jurisdiction associates with a lawyer licensed to practice in this jurisdiction. For this paragraph to apply, however, the lawyer admitted to practice in this jurisdiction must actively participate in and share responsibility for the representation of the client.

Lawyers not admitted to practice generally in a jurisdiction may be authorized by law or order of a tribunal or an administrative agency to appear before the tribunal or agency. This authority may be granted pursuant to formal rules governing admission pro hac vice or pursuant to informal practice of the tribunal or agency. Under paragraph (c) (2), a lawyer does not violate this Rule when the lawyer appears before a tribunal or agency pursuant to such authority. To the extent that a court rule or other law of this jurisdiction requires a lawyer who is not admitted to practice in this jurisdiction to obtain admission pro hac vice before appearing before a tribunal or administrative agency, this Rule requires the lawyer to obtain that authority.

Paragraph (c) (2) also provides that a lawyer rendering services in this jurisdiction on a temporary basis does not violate this Rule when the lawyer engages in conduct in anticipation of a proceeding or hearing in a jurisdiction in which the lawyer is authorized to practice law or in which the lawyer reasonably expects to be admitted pro hac vice. Examples of such conduct include meetings with the client, interviews of potential witnesses, and the review of documents. Similarly, a lawyer admitted only in another jurisdiction may engage in conduct temporarily in this jurisdiction in connection with pending litigation in another jurisdiction in which the lawyer is or reasonably expects to be authorized to appear, including taking depositions in this jurisdiction.

When a lawyer has been or reasonably expects to be admitted to appear before a court or administrative agency, paragraph (c)(2) also permits conduct by lawyers who are associated with that lawyer in the matter, but who do not expect to appear before the court or administrative agency. For example, subordinate lawyers may conduct research, review documents, and attend meetings with witnesses in support of the lawyer responsible for the litigation.

 Paragraph (c) (3) permits a lawyer admitted to practice law in another jurisdiction to perform services on a temporary basis in this jurisdiction if those services are in or reasonably related to a pending or potential arbitration, mediation, or other alternative dispute resolution proceeding in this or another jurisdiction, if the services arise out of or are reasonably related to the lawyer's practice in a jurisdiction in which the lawyer is admitted to practice. The lawyer, however, must obtain admission pro hac vice in the case of a court-annexed arbitration or mediation or otherwise if court rules or law so require.

Paragraph (c)(4) permits a lawyer admitted in another jurisdiction to provide certain legal services on a temporary basis in this jurisdiction that arise out of or are reasonably related to the lawyer's practice in a jurisdiction in which the lawyer is admitted but are not within paragraphs (c)(2) or (c)(3). These services include both legal services and services that nonlawyers may perform but that are considered the practice of law when performed by lawyers.

Paragraphs (c) (3) and (c) (4) require that the services arise out of or be reasonably related to the lawyer's practice in a jurisdiction in which the lawyer is admitted. A variety of factors evidence such a relationship. The lawyer's client may have been previously represented by the lawyer, or may be resident in or have substantial contacts with the jurisdiction in which the lawyer is admitted. The matter, although involving other jurisdictions, may have a significant connection with that jurisdiction. In other cases, significant aspects of the lawyer's work might be conducted in that jurisdiction or a significant aspect of the matter may involve the law of that jurisdiction. The necessary relationship might arise when the client's activities or the legal issues involve multiple jurisdictions, such as when the officers of a multinational corporation survey potential business sites and seek the services of their lawyer in assessing the relative merits of each. In addition, the services may draw on the lawyer's recognized expertise developed through the regular practice of law on behalf of clients in matters involving a particular body of federal, nationally-uniform, foreign, or international law. Lawyers desiring to provide *pro bono* legal services on a temporary basis in a jurisdiction that has been affected by a major disaster, but in which they are not otherwise authorized to practice law, as well as lawyers from the affected jurisdiction who seek to practice law temporarily in another jurisdiction, but in which they are not otherwise authorized to practice law, should consult the [Model *Court Rule on Provision of Legal Services Following Determination of Major Disaster*].

Paragraph (d) identifies two circumstances in which a lawyer who is admitted to practice in another United States jurisdiction, and is not disbarred or suspended from practice in any jurisdiction, may establish an office or other systematic and continuous presence in this jurisdiction for the practice of law as well as provide legal services on a temporary basis. Except as provided in paragraphs (d) (1) and (d) (2), a lawyer who is admitted to practice law in another jurisdiction and who establishes an office or other systematic or continuous presence in this jurisdiction must become admitted to practice law generally in this jurisdiction.

Paragraph (d)(1) applies to a lawyer who is employed by a client to provide legal services to the client or its organizational affiliates, i.e., entities that control, are controlled by, or are under common control with the employer. This paragraph does not authorize the provision of personal legal services to the employer's officers or employees. The paragraph applies to in-house corporate lawyers, government lawyers and others who are employed to render legal services to the employer. The lawyer's ability to represent the employer outside the jurisdiction in which the lawyer is licensed generally serves the interests of the employer and does not create an unreasonable risk to the client and others because the employer is well situated to assess the lawyer's qualifications and the quality of the lawyer's work.

If an employed lawyer establishes an office or other systematic presence in this jurisdiction for the purpose of rendering legal services to the employer, the lawyer may be subject to registration or other requirements, including assessments for client protection funds and mandatory continuing legal education.

Paragraph (d)(2) recognizes that a lawyer may provide legal services in a jurisdiction in which the lawyer is not licensed when authorized to do so by federal or other law, which includes statute, court rule, executive regulation or judicial precedent.

A lawyer who practices law in this jurisdiction pursuant to paragraphs (c) or (d) or otherwise is subject to the disciplinary authority of this jurisdiction. See Rule 8.5(a).

In some circumstances, a lawyer who practices law in this jurisdiction pursuant to paragraphs (c) or (d) may have to inform the client that the lawyer is not licensed to practice law in this jurisdiction. For example, that may be required when the representation occurs primarily in this jurisdiction and requires knowledge of the law of this jurisdiction. See Rule 1.4(b).

Paragraphs (c) and (d) do not authorize communications advertising legal services to prospective clients in this jurisdiction by lawyers who are admitted to practice in other jurisdictions. Whether and how lawyers may communicate the availability of their services to prospective clients in this jurisdiction is governed by Rules 7.1 to

Partnering with Colleagues and Case Referrals

Certain ethical rules deserve special attention in regard to the issue of referring cases and taking referrals, beginning with Model Rule 1.1: Competence. The rule states: "A lawyer shall provide competent representation to a client. Competent representation requires the legal knowledge, skill, thoroughness and preparation reasonably necessary for the representation." Lawyers often refer cases when the matter is outside their area of expertise, the right thing to do.

The Comments to Model Rule 1.1 are instructive: "A lawyer can provide adequate representation in a wholly novel field through necessary study." The better practice, however, is to do what you know how to do. When your expertise is overwhelmed, referrals are preferable to "necessary study." The decision to refer, however, is not the end of a lawyer's responsibility, but, rather, a beginning. And when referring a case, do your homework. Make certain that the lawyer you are sending the client to for representation has sufficient expertise in the relevant area of law to provide the client with competent representation. This single failure has taken many lawyers into the world of malpractice claims based on an allegation of "negligent referral."

Model Rule 1.5 has particular relevance to the issue of file referral where a division of fees is involved. Model Rule 1.5(e) states:

(e) A division of a fee between lawyers who are not in the same firm may be made only if:

(1) the division is in proportion to the services performed by each lawyer, or each lawyer assumes joint responsibility for the representation;

(2) the client agrees to the arrangement, including the share each lawyer will receive, and the agreement is confirmed in writing; and

(3) the total fee is reasonable.

The retainer agreement in referral cases is most often drafted by the lawyer receiving the referral. In those cases, there can be a tendency and a temptation to omit the referring lawyer's name from the agreement. Often, the referring lawyer is a friend of the client or they share a past relationship whereby the referring lawyer does not want the client to be aware of the financial relationship that the referral has created. Similarly, the referral lawyer (whose competency has been praised by the referring lawyer to the client to encourage the relationship in the first place) may not want the client to know that a fee will follow the praise. These are innocent facts if dealt with up front; they are hard to explain if discovered later, after things have potentially not gone so well. Always be up front and complete when describing this relationship to the client. Model Rule 1.5(e) requires the agreement to be in writing. Make certain to include the name of the referring lawyer on the retainer agreement and document in the retainer agreement the basis for the fee-splitting arrangement. The client is likely to read the retainer agreement carefully, while less attention might be paid to other correspondence generated during the normal course of a case.

Ethical Advertising and the Pitfalls in Online Marketing

Lawyers may participate in both not-for-profit and for-profit lawyer Internet-based referral services where the services require a flat fee for participation, a flat fee for transmitting the lawyer's name to a potential client, and/or a flat fee for every client secured as a result of a referral.

Applicable Rules

• Rule 5.4 (Professional Independence of a Lawyer)

• Rule 7.1 (Communications Regarding a Lawyer's Services)

Inquiry

We have received a number of inquiries concerning participation in, and the creation of, Internet-based referral services. All inquires seek guidance on whether a lawyer's participation in a specific program would be permissible under the D.C. Rules of Professional Conduct. Specifically, we have been asked to provide guidance with respect to the applicability of D.C. Rules 5.4 and 7.1 to lawyer participation in referral services under the terms common to the programs reviewed.

Most referral programs are run by State Bar Associations or other nonprofit organizations. There are, however, a substantial number of programs that are operated by for-profit organizations, and these services vary in size, sophistication, legal specialty, and design. While most sites have numerous disclaimers that could be accessed from the home page, the cost of lawyer participation and the existence of fees required if a lawyer is selected through the referral service are often not apparent without signing up for the service.

The common elements among the inquiries included the following: (1) the services do not charge a fee to the prospective client or consumer; (2) they charge, instead, a flat fee for lawyers to participate in the service; (3) they require that the fees charged by the lawyers to clients secured through the referral service not be higher than fees charged to clients who do not use the referral service; (4) they provide guidelines on the type of information that participating lawyers must provide; (5) they adopt specific qualification requirements for lawyers to participate (e.g., certificates of specialties, malpractice insurance, minimum number of years of practice); (6) they include disclaimers to prospective clients that the lawyer is responsible for the content of the description of the lawyer's services; and (7) they provide disclaimers stating that the referral service does not provide legal advice or recommend a particular lawyer. In addition, none of the referral services reviewed appear to solicit prospective clients by "in-person contact."[1] While the referral services advertise in a variety of media, the consumer or the prospective client must initiate the contact with the referral service to receive any referrals.

Background

Rule 7.1 of the D.C. Rules of Professional Conduct governs all communications regarding a lawyer's services, including advertising. The Rule prohibits a lawyer from making a false or misleading communication about her services and imposes certain limits on in-person solicitation.

Prior to February 1, 2007, D.C. Rule 7.1(b) permitted lawyers to use paid intermediaries to make in-person contact with prospective clients, so long as the lawyer reasonably knew that such solicitation was consistent with the intermediary's contractual or other legal obligations and the lawyer took reasonable steps to ensure that the potential client was informed about how much the intermediary was paid and the effect, if any, of the payment on the lawyer's total fee. The current version of D.C. Rule 7.1(b) no longer permits the use of paid intermediaries. "A lawyer shall not give anything of value to a person (other than the lawyer's partner or employee) for recommending the lawyer's services through in-person contact." D.C. Rule 7.1(b) (2). Comment [5] explicitly states that a "lawyer is no longer permitted to conduct in-person solicitation through the use of a paid intermediary."

The District of Columbia Bar Rules of Professional Conduct Review Committee recommended this change for two reasons:

First, lawyer advertising in now widespread, reaching diverse communities in the District of Columbia, including non-English speakers and immigrants. Concerns that certain persons, without the intervention of a paid intermediary, would be unable to locate a lawyer to hire, should no longer exist. Second, there is reason to believe that at least some paid intermediaries, who are effectively beyond the power of the Bar to regulate, have used harassing, abusive, or unseemly practices in soliciting potential clients for lawyers.

District of Columbia Bar Rules of Professional Conduct Review Committee, *Proposed Amendments to the District to Columbia Rules of Professional Conduct: Final Report and Recommendations (Clean*

Copy) 179 (June 21, 2005; revised Oct. 6, 2005).

While we have not previously addressed an inquiry about Internet-based referral services that charge lawyers a fee for participating, we have addressed similar or analogous inquires. All of those inquiries have been resolved, at least in part, with references to the now prohibited practice of using paid intermediaries. *See, e.g.,* D.C. Ethics Ops. 261 (1995), 286 (1998), 302 (2000), & 307 (2001). Thus, our conclusions reached in these prior opinions must be read and reassessed in light of the recent amendments to D.C. Rule 7.1.

There are three principal differences between the Model Rules (and those of other jurisdictions) and D.C. Rule 7.1 that are relevant to the inquiries. First, D.C. Rule 7.1 is more permissive than the Model Rule with respect to lawyer solicitation. Model Rule 7.3 generally prohibits a lawyer from engaging in any in-person solicitation of potential clients (which the Model Rules define to include both live telephone calls and "real-time electronic contact") unless the potential client is either a lawyer or has a pre-existing relationship with the contacting lawyer. By contrast, in the District of Columbia, Rule 7.1 permits a lawyer to make such in-person solicitations so long as the lawyer's claims are not misleading, the solicitation does not involve the use of coercion, duress, or harassment, and the potential client has the capacity to make reasoned judgments regarding the selection of a lawyer. *See* D.C. Rule 7.1(b).[4]

Second, the D.C. Rule 7.1 is less restrictive than other jurisdictions in regulating advertising. The rule only requires that advertising not contain misrepresentations of fact or law or assertions that cannot be substantiated. *See* D.C. Rule 7.1(a). Comment [4] further states that any restrictions beyond these limited requirements impose barriers to the flow of information about lawyers' services. Although Model Rule 7.2 is similar in this regard, other jurisdictions are much more restrictive. *See, e.g.,* Iowa Rule of Professional Conduct 32:7.2 Advertising.

Finally, D.C. Rule 7.1 differs from the Model Rule regarding participation in lawyer referral programs. Both rules now prohibit a lawyer from paying a person to recommend her services (*e.g.,* intermediaries), and both rules carve out an exception for referral services. Model Rule 7.2, however, states that a lawyer may "pay the usual charges of … *a not-for-profit or qualified lawyer referral service*" (emphasis added). A "qualified lawyer referral service" is defined as one that "has been approved by an appropriate regulatory authority." Model Rule 7.2(b) (2). Comment [6] to D.C. Rule

7.1, on the other hand, simply states that "a lawyer may participate in lawyer referral programs and pay the usual fees charged by such programs." Thus, the D.C. Rule, which was adapted from the Model Rule, specifically omitted wording that would limit payment of fees only to not-for-profit referral services or to services that are otherwise regulated by appropriate authorities.

Discussion

In the District of Columbia, questions regarding a lawyer's participation in an Internet-based referral service are no different than any other question about lawyer communications regarding legal services. We have previously said that "we see nothing untoward in lawyers communicating about their services through web sites, provided that such communications comply with our general rules governing lawyer communications with clients." D.C. Ethics Op. 302. Such communications are governed by D.C. Rule 7.1.

As an initial matter, the rule requires lawyers to ensure that their listings with the referral services, and any statements made by the referral services about the lawyers' services, satisfy D.C. Rule 7.1(a). Thus, the lawyers must ensure that the communications about their services provided by the referral service are neither false nor misleading and that any affirmative statements about their legal services can be substantiated. *See* D.C. Ethics Op. 249 (1994). The referral programs under review request information such as the following: office locations; contact information; years of practice; certificates of specialty if the State Bar recognizes specializations; current areas of practice; certificate of malpractice insurance; and current bar memberships. Our rules expressly permit the public dissemination of this type of information.

The referral service must also conform to the requirements of D.C. Rule 7.1(b) (2), which prohibits a lawyer from giving "anything of value to a person (other than the lawyer's partner or employee) for recommending the lawyer's services through in-person contact." As previously discussed, this language was added to make clear that use of paid intermediaries in the District of Columbia is now prohibited. Notwithstanding this change to the text of the rule, the relevant language in the Comments remains unchanged, and it states that "a lawyer may participate in lawyer referral programs and pay the usual fees charged by such a programs." D.C. Rule 7.1, Comment [6]. Thus, Rule 7.1(b) (2) was not intended to curtail participation in fee charging referral programs, but, rather, to stop lawyers from using paid intermediaries to make in-person solicitations. The key distinction between referral programs and paid intermediaries is that referral programs do not generally engage in unsolicited in-person contact with prospective clients.

Each of the referral programs described by the inquirers requires that the prospective client initiate contact with the referral service to receive any information about a prospective lawyer. While the referral services advertise through websites and other media outlets, none of them initiates unsolicited in-person communications with prospective clients. Instead, the inquirers all described Internet-based services through which prospective clients can electronically request a referral. For some services, the prospective client can call the referral service for technical assistance in using the web site to request a referral. Others allow the prospective client to either submit the request electronically, or call the service to receive referrals. But none of the services engage in any unsolicited contact with prospective clients.

Each referral service also informs the prospective client that the service is simply providing a list of available lawyers and is not recommending any particular lawyer. In many cases, the service provides multiple random referrals for each request. While the particular programs described in the inquiries we received do not recommend any specific lawyers when they transmit the names to potential clients, we do not believe that our conclusions would change if these programs were to make specific recommendations. Such recommendations would, however, be subject to scrutiny under Rule 7.1(a). Specifically, we believe that a service that recommends a lawyer without offering any explanation of the basis for the recommendation could be misleading, particularly if the service simply recommends any lawyer who pays a fee. However, if the basis for the recommendation is clearly explained, such advertising is unlikely to run afoul of Rule 7.1(a).

With respect to fees, the programs described by the inquirers require of each lawyer a flat fee to participate or to have information listed with the service for a specified period of time. Such fees are permissible if they are "the usual fees charged by such programs." D.C. Rule 7.1, Comment [6]. What is "usual" will vary over time and among different services based on the costs of operating them. At a minimum, "usual" means that the fees fall within a range of fees charged by comparable services.

D.C. Rule 5.4 generally prohibits lawyers from "sharing" fees with nonlawyers. The purpose of this prohibition is to "protect the lawyer's professional independence of judgment." D.C. Rule 5.4,

Comment [1]. Although some of the referral programs make the payment of a fee contingent upon securing a client from the referral, none of them makes the fee contingent on the outcome of the case or on the amount of the legal fees. As we explained in Opinion 286, "[a] non-contingent payment for the referral of legal business, *i.e.*, one that is paid regardless of the success or outcome of the representation, is not a division of legal fees. Such payments are simply part of a lawyer's marketing expenses, payable whether or not they produce revenue for the lawyer." Thus, we conclude that a flat fee for transmittals, or for each client secured, does not violate either D.C. Rule 7.1 or 5.4.

In Opinion 307, we considered a referral system operated by the federal government. That referral program required that a law firm bidding to participate on a schedule contract to provide legal services to a government agency pay one percent of the fee income generated in order to cover the costs of the referral program. We concluded that

the drafters of the D.C. Rules were not particularly concerned about the manner in which non-profit lawyer referral services structured their fee arrangements; their principal focus was on preventing non-lawyer intermediaries from using their power over lawyers who rely on them for business referrals to influence those lawyers' "professional independence of judgment." D.C. Rule 5.4, Comment [1].

We went on to recognize that "the development of referral schemes that do not compromise lawyers' independence [is] a positive development, though we recognize that our Rules are less clear than they could be on this issue." D.C. Ethics Op. 307. The recent amendments to D.C. Rule 5.4 now expressly allow a lawyer to share legal fees "with a nonprofit organization that employed, retained, or recommended employment of the lawyer in the matter and that qualifies under Section 501(c)(3) of the Internal Revenue Code." D.C. Rule 5.4(a) (5).

 Thus, while there is no distinction between not-for-profit and for-profit referral services in D.C. Rule 7.1, D.C. Rule 5.4 does make a distinction between not-for-profit and for-profit programs with respect to fee sharing. But as long as the lawyers participating in a for-profit Internet-based referral program pay a flat fee, or a flat fee per transmittal, rather than a portion of the fees earned from the client, D.C. Rule 5.4 is not violated.

Finally, all of the inquiries we received made clear that none of the participating lawyers would have any financial interest in the referral service. Nor would any participating lawyer have any employment or contractual relationship with the referral service provider even where the provider was a large entity with other business interests. If such a relationship were to exist, it would likely prove problematic under D.C. Rule 5.4(b).

In sum, the amended D.C. Rules prohibit a lawyer from conducting, "in-person solicitation through the use of a paid intermediary," but allow a lawyer to "participate in lawyer referral programs and pay the usual fees charged by such programs." *See* D.C. Rule 7.1, Comments [5] and [6]. Thus, we conclude that participation in lawyer referral programs, like those described above, that conform to the D.C. Rules of Professional Conduct in general, and to D.C. Rules 7.1 and 5.4 in particular, is permitted.

Published: November 2007

"In-person contact" or solicitation "includes[s] telephone contact but not electronic mail." D.C. Rule 7.1, Comment [5].

 As amended, D.C. Rule 7.1 states in pertinent part that:

(a) A lawyer shall not make a false or misleading communication about the lawyer or the lawyer's services. A communication is false or misleading if it: (1) Contains a material misrepresentation of fact or law, or omits a fact necessary to make the statement considered as a whole not materially misleading; or

(2) Contains an assertion about the lawyer or the lawyer's services that cannot be substantiated.

(b) (1) A lawyer shall not seek by in-person contact, employment (or employment of a partner or associate) by a nonlawyer who has not sought the lawyer's advice regarding employment of a lawyer, if:

(A) The solicitation involves use of a statement or claim that is false or misleading, within the meaning of paragraph (a);

(B) The solicitation involves the use of coercion, duress or harassment; or

(C) The potential client is apparently in a physical or mental condition which would make it unlikely that the potential client could exercise reasonable, considered judgment as to the selection of a lawyer.

(2) A lawyer shall not give anything of value to a person (other than the lawyer's partner or employee) for recommending the lawyer's services through in-person contact.

(c) A lawyer shall not knowingly assist an organization that furnishes or pays for legal services to others to promote the use of the lawyer's services or those of the lawyer's partner or associate, or any other lawyer affiliated with the lawyer or the lawyer's firm, as a private practitioner, if the promotional activity involves the use of coercion, duress, compulsion, intimidation, threats, or vexatious or harassing conduct.

The prior version of D.C. Rule 7.1 included the following language:

(b) A lawyer shall not seek by in-person contact or through an intermediary, employment (or employment of a partner or associate) by a nonlawyer who has not sought the lawyer's advice regarding employment of a lawyer, if:

. . . .

(4) The solicitation involves use of an intermediary and the lawyer knows or could reasonably ascertain that such conduct violates the intermediary's contractual or other legal obligations; or

(5) The solicitation involves the use of an intermediary and the lawyer has not taken all reasonable steps to ensure that the potential client is informed of (a) the consideration, if any, paid or to be paid by the lawyer to the intermediary, and (b) the effect, if any, of the payment to the intermediary on the total fee to be charged.

Lawyers should be aware that substantive law may limit certain solicitation practices in particular circumstances. *See, e.g.*, D.C. Code § 22-3225.14 (limiting the ability of lawyers and other "practitioners," whether directly or through a paid intermediary, to solicit clients during the 21-day period following a motor vehicle accident).

Because the Internet crosses jurisdictional boundaries, and because we rely on unique aspects of the District of Columbia Rules, lawyers who accept referrals should exercise particular care when doing so from clients based in, or regarding matters arising out of, other jurisdictions, because the rules of those jurisdictions may apply. *See* D.C. Rule 8.5(b), D.C. Ethics Op. 311 (2002).

"This rule permits public dissemination of information concerning a lawyer's name or firm name, address, and telephone number; the kinds of services the lawyer will undertake; the basis on which the lawyer's fees are determined, including prices for specific services and payment and credit arrangements; a lawyer's foreign language ability; names of references and, with their consent, names of clients regularly represented; and other information that might invite the attention of those seeking legal assistance." D.C. Rule 7.1, Comment [3].

Because most of these services allow referrals to be made over the telephone, the communications arguably fall within the definition of "in-person" solicitation under the D.C. Rules. But we interpret the prohibition in D.C. Rule 7.1(b)(2) against paying a person for recommending the lawyer's services through in-person contact not to extend to situations in which a prospective client makes a telephone call to a referral service and affirmatively requests a name or names of lawyers. We do not believe that D.C. Rule 7.1(b) (2) was intended to prohibit a lawyer from paying to participate in a referral service in which the prospective client initiates the contact, expressly seeking lawyer referrals.

The location of such an explanation is likely to vary from web site to web site depending on the design. We have cautioned before that, "because web pages allow multi-layered communications, questions may arise about whether a visitor to a web page may be misled because relevant disclosures are hidden many clicks away from the main pages." D.C. Ethics Op. 302.

Opinion 286, along with other opinions discussing payments of fees for referrals (*see, e.g.*, D.C. Ethics Op. 307), incorporated into its analysis of fee sharing an analysis of the District of Columbia's unique rule permitting the use of intermediaries. While the rule no longer permits the use of intermediaries, the reasoning of these opinions with respect to fee sharing remains sound.

The rule change only addressed nonprofit organizations that qualify under section 501(c) (3); Opinion 307 continues to apply with respect to *government* referral services.

Assisting a Pro-Se Litigant

In ABA Formal Opinion 07-446 *Undisclosed Legal Assistance to Pro Se Litigants* (2007), the ABA Standing Committee on Ethics and Professional Responsibility stated that lawyers can furnish such assistance without disclosing to the court or to the opposing party that they had done so provided that the failure to disclose would not amount to fraudulent or dishonest conduct by clients. The opinion stated:

Whether the lawyer must see to it that the client makes some disclosure to the tribunal (or makes some disclosure independently) depends on whether the fact of assistance is material to the matter, that is, whether the failure to disclose that fact would constitute fraudulent or otherwise dishonest conduct on the part of the client, thereby involving the lawyer in conduct violative of Rules 1.2(d), 3.3(b), 4.1(b), or 8.4(c). In our opinion, the fact that a litigant submitting papers to a tribunal on a pro se basis has received legal assistance behind the scenes is not material to the merits of the litigation.

The committee noted that such assistance is a form of "unbundling" whereby a lawyer performs a limited set of tasks relating to the representation under Model Rule 1.2(c) as opposed to handling all aspects of a matter.

The committee stated that some of the arguments advanced against allowing lawyers to provide such assistance include the concern that *pro se* litigants are accorded special treatment by the court, so that to permit lawyers to provide such assistance without notifying the court would result in an unfair advantage for the litigant. The committee found this to be without merit, since it would be obvious on the face of the pleadings as to whether a lawyer was involved. Furthermore, the committee noted, the fact that the litigant has received assistance should not result in an unfair advantage simply because pleadings filed with the court must pass muster on their own merit:

…A court that refuses to dismiss or enter summary judgment against a non ghostwritten *pro se* pleading that lacks essential facts or elements commits reversible error in the same manner as if it refuses to deny such dispositive motions against an attorney-drafted complaint – Goldschmidt, In Defense of Ghostwriting, 29 Fordham Urb. L.J. 1145 (2002)

Finally, the committee noted that the lawyer would not be acting dishonestly in providing such assistance unless the client was to "make a statement that could be attributed to the lawyer that the documents were prepared without legal assistance.

What to Do when you are Way over your Head

The Rules of Professional Conduct are rules of reason. They should be interpreted with reference to the purposes of legal representation and of the law itself. Some of the Rules are imperatives; cast in the terms "shall" or "shall not." These define proper conduct for purposes of professional discipline. Others, generally cast in the term "may," are permissive and define areas under the Rules in which the lawyer has discretion to exercise professional judgment. No disciplinary action should be taken when the lawyer chooses not to act or acts within the bounds of such discretion. Other Rules define the nature of relationships between the lawyer and others. The Rules are thus partly obligatory and disciplinary and partly constitutive and descriptive in that they define a lawyer's professional role. Many of the Comments use the term "should." Comments do not add obligations to the Rules but provide guidance for practicing in compliance with the Rules.

The Rules presuppose a larger legal context shaping the lawyer's role. That context includes court rules and statutes relating to matters of licensure, laws defining specific obligations of lawyers and substantive and procedural law in general. The Comments are sometimes used to alert lawyers to their responsibilities under such other law.

Compliance with the Rules, as with all law in an open society, depends primarily upon understanding and voluntary compliance, secondarily upon reinforcement by peer and public opinion and finally, when necessary, upon enforcement through disciplinary proceedings. The Rules do not, however, exhaust the moral and ethical considerations that should inform a lawyer, for no worthwhile human activity can be completely defined by legal rules. The Rules simply provide a framework for the ethical practice of law.

Violation of a Rule should not itself give rise to a cause of action against a lawyer nor should it create any presumption in such a case that a legal duty has been breached. In addition, violation of a Rule does not necessarily warrant any other nondisciplinary remedy, such as disqualification of a lawyer in pending litigation. The Rules are designed to provide guidance to lawyers and to provide a structure for regulating conduct through disciplinary agencies. They are not designed to be a basis for civil liability. Furthermore, the purpose of the Rules can be subverted when they are invoked by opposing parties as procedural weapons. The fact that a Rule is a just basis for a lawyer's self-assessment, or for sanctioning a lawyer under the administration of a disciplinary authority, does not imply that an antagonist in a collateral proceeding or transaction has standing to seek enforcement of the Rule. Nevertheless, since the Rules do establish standards of conduct by lawyers, a lawyer's violation of a Rule may be evidence of breach of the applicable standard of conduct.

Hidden Dangers of Office Sharing Arrangements

Sharing Office Space and Services by Unaffiliated Lawyers

Unaffiliated lawyers may share office space and related services so long as the arrangements for such sharing do not compromise the confidentiality of each attorney's client information, the independence of each attorney, and the separate obligations of each attorney to comply with the Rules of Professional Conduct. In addition, the sharing arrangements must be structured in a way that does not suggest to the public that the lawyers are affiliated when they are not.

Applicable Rules

- Rule 1.6 (Confidentiality of Information)
- Rule 1.7 (Conflicts of Interest)
- Rule 1.10 (Imputed Disqualification)
- Rule 7.1 (Communications Concerning Lawyer's Services)
- Rule 7.5 (Firm Names and Letterheads)

There is litigation in the area where an attorney shares office space with another attorney and the client makes a false assumption that the other attorney is a member of the firm. In most cases, the suits are civil suits as opposed to the discipline of a Bar Association.

www.ingramcontent.com/pod-product-compliance
Lightning Source LLC
Chambersburg PA
CBHW081550170526
45166CB00009B/2652